W. R. Rodgers

Title	*Author*
SEAN O'CASEY	Bernard Benstock
J. C. MANGAN	James Kilroy
STANDISH O'GRADY	Phillip L. Marcus
AUSTIN CLARKE	John Jordan
BRIAN FRIEL	D. E. S. Maxwell
DANIEL CORKERY	George Brandon Saul
EIMAR O'DUFFY	Robert Hogan
FRANK O'CONNOR	James Matthews
GEORGE MOORE	Janet Egleson
JAMES JOYCE	Fritz Senn
JOHN BUTLER YEATS	Douglas Archibald
LORD EDWARD DUNSANY	Zack Bowen
MARIA EDGEWORTH	James Newcomer
MARY LAVIN	Zack Bowen
OSCAR WILDE	Edward Partridge
PAUL VINCENT CARROLL	Paul A. Doyle
SEUMAS O'KELLY	George Brandon Saul
SHERIDAN LeFANU	Michael Begnal
SOMERVILLE AND ROSS	John Cronin
SUSAN MITCHELL	Richard M. Kain
J. M. SYNGE	Robin Skelton
KATHARINE TYNAN	Marilyn Gaddis Rose
LIAM O'FLAHERTY	James O'Brien
IRIS MURDOCH	Donna Gerstenberger

W. R. RODGERS
(1909-1969)

Darcy O'Brien

Lewisburg
BUCKNELL UNIVERSITY PRESS

© 1970 by Associated University Presses, Inc.
Library of Congress Catalogue Card Number: 70-124646

Associated University Presses, Inc.
Cranbury, New Jersey 08512

ISBN: 0-8387-7750-3 (cloth edition)
0-8387-7630-2 (paper)
Printed in the United States of America

Contents

Contents

Introduction

On September 9, 1968, the Dublin Arts Council granted W. R. Rodgers a £100 annuity "as an acknowledgment of your distinction in letters and of the honour which your literary work has reflected on this country." It is a pity that the award could not have come sooner, for Rodgers lived long enough to collect only £100. The Arts Council was paying tribute to his accomplishments as a poet and as a broadcaster. The number of his poems is relatively small—seventy or so in all—but their quality is uniformly high and a few of them can be called great. When his second volume of verse appeared in 1952, he was ranked with Louis MacNeice, Patrick Kavanagh and Austin Clarke among the finest Irish poets then writing. In his other role, as a producer, writer and broadcaster for the B.B.C., he became the oral historian of the Irish literary movement and a familiar voice for twenty years, talking about other Irish writers, telling stories, and reading his own poems.

Whether knowing a writer makes one a better or worse judge of his works is debatable. But as I knew Bertie Rodgers during the last two and a half years of his life, I have had no choice but to accept that advantage or handicap in the writing of this little book. I recall one biographer of an American writer who avoided meeting his subject for fear it would cloud his judgment. He waited for the man to drop dead and then set about getting to know him objectively through his letters, friends and widows. But Rodgers came to live and die in my town before I had ever thought of writing about him, so I did not get a chance to worry about the problem.

It was only after I had watched his ashes disappear into the ground at Loughgall, County Armagh, where he had been the Presbyterian minister for twelve years, only after I had seen the landscape of his poems and heard about him from his friends and family that I began to want to write about him. He was often a secretly private poet. By that I mean that many ostensibly impersonal poems emerged from personal experience. He wrote about things he had seen and felt, and when he did turn to the more abstract subjects of religion and myth, he smoked them in his own pipe. For that reason, I think it is necessary to know something of his Ireland and of his personality to appreciate his verse fully. For myself, I can say that reading his poems is a greater pleasure to me now than when I was ignorant of these things.

I wish I had known him longer, for my sake and for the sake of this book. But I have tried to fill in the gaps by listening to his family and friends, by gathering what printed information I could, and by listening to what tapes exist of his B.B.C. broadcasts. Mrs. Marianne Rodgers, his widow, has been entirely generous in talking to me, showing me Rodgers's personal papers, including unpublished essays and dream-books, and in permitting me to quote from his works. Mrs. Reah Purefoy of Dublin, Rodgers's twin sister, has been no less generous, helping me in particular with the Belfast and Loughgall periods of his life. I wish to thank them both and to express the hope that they and Rodgers's daughters, Mrs. Harden Rodgers Jay of Dublin, and Miss Nini Rodgers of Belfast, together with his younger sister, Mrs. Jean McMaster of Hillsborough, County Down, find this book a worthy memorial.

I am grateful also to Mr. John Boyd of the B.B.C., Belfast for supplying me with a transcript of *The Return Room*; to Mr. Tom Hart of West Lavington, Sussex, for a copy of *Essex Roundabout*; and to Mr. Bert Meyers of Claremont, California, for permission to quote the text of his poem in memory of Rodgers.

Acknowledgments are due to Secker & Warburg, to Harcourt, Brace, and to Farrar, Straus and Giroux for permission to quote from *Awake*! and *Europa and the Bull*.

Chronology

1909: Born William Robert Rodgers, August 1, Belfast.

1931: B.A. Degree from Queen's University, Belfast.

1935: Ordained and installed as Presbyterian minister at Loughgall, County Armagh.

1936: Marries Marie (born Mary) Harden Waddell.

1939: Harden born.

1941: Nini born; *Awake! And other poems* published; first visit to Dublin.

1942: American edition of *Awake!*

1943–
  44: Resides in Oxford; "Black North" published in the *New Statesman and Nation*.

1945: Meets Marianne Helweg Gilliam; "Lent" published.

1946: Resigns from ministry to take B.B.C. job in London.

1948: "W.B. Yeats," his first radio portrait, is broadcast.

1951: Elected to Irish Academy of Letters.

1952: *Europa and the Bull* published in England and America.

1953: Marie Harden Waddell Rodgers dies; marries Marianne Helweg; moves to Stoke-by-Nayland, Essex.

1954: Moves to Borley, Suffolk.

1955: *The Return Room* broadcast.

1956: Lucy born.

1957: *Ireland in Colour* published.

1959: Moves to Ardleigh, Essex.

1963: *Essex Roundabout* published; moves to Colchester.

1965: Last radio portrait, "AE," broadcast.

1966: Last program for B.B.C., "Old Ireland Free"; *Return Room* rebroadcast; moves to Claremont, California, and assumes post as Writer in Residence, Pitzer College.

1968: Presents Irish Festival in Claremont; awarded annual stipend by Dublin Arts Council; awarded grant by Chapelbrook Foundation to edit his broadcasts for publication; assumes post at California State Polytechnic College.

1969: Dies February 1, Los Angeles; buried in Loughgall, County Armagh, March 7; *Return Room* rebroadcast.

W. R. Rodgers

1

The Return Room

In America if a man is a poet we peek under the rugs of his childhood to find out what made him so. Something queer must be secreted there. In Ireland why a man becomes a poet is a question not to be asked. It is the only Irish question free of mystery. "Mad Ireland hurt you into poetry," said Auden of Yeats. That says enough. Think of Conor Cruise O'Brien's definition of what constitutes an Irishman—"Irishness is not primarily a question of birth or blood or language: it is the condition of being involved in the Irish situation, and usually of being mauled by it"—and understand why there has never been any difficulty filling the quota of 1,400 Irish poets established at Druim Ceat in the 6th century A.D.

An Irish mauling can take many forms. For Joyce it was a father, a mother, and a Church; for Frank O'Connor, a father, a mother, and a war; for Patrick Kavanagh, the "stony grey soil of Monaghan," which bore him his great hunger. For W. R. Rodgers it was the "hug-

me-tight" of Northern holiness and his own life-long
squirming and yielding, yielding and squirming, within that snug embrace.

> Humdrummery of history:
> Three hundred years ago my foundling fathers
> With farthing fists, and thistles in their eyes
> Were wished upon this foreshore;
> Bibles for bibs and bloody pikes for rattles,
> And tombs for keeps. There was not time
> To wade through wedding to a birth:
> The God of battles took the banns for read,
> Calvin and culverin sang the cradle song
> And Cromwell made the bed:
> Put to a frugal breast of swollen hopes
> They did their levelling best.

Such was the way Rodgers imagined his forebears. He
knew himself to be "heir to all that Adamnation and
hand-me-down of doom." The Irishman gets mauled
because his is a land of clashes and contraries, with
reconciliations rarer than white blackbirds. And if you
are a Belfast lad, as Bertie Rodgers was, you hear the
street-rhyme,

> Up a long ladder and down a short rope
> Away with King Billy and God bless the Pope,

and its proper riposte,

> King Billy was a gentleman,
> He wore a watch and chain,
> The Pope he was a beggar man
> And lived in Chapel Lane.

And you know which side of the street to run to.
These are but children's taunts, but their elders have

other ways of taunting. In Belfast, Churchill is said to have said, they do everything but eat the bodies.

Rodgers's childhood spanned the years of the Easter Rising, the Irish war for independence, and the Irish civil war, which was fought over the question of whether six Northern counties should remain British. Violent times. The street-warfare in Belfast in 1969 can give us an idea of that aspect of Rodgers's youth. Every night his father would spread open the *Belfast Telegraph* and scan the list of casualties. "Woman dear," he would say to his wife, "this is terrible. Eight Catholics. Nine Protestants." And the family would shrink from the window at the crackle of distant rifle-fire. But the next night Justice would right the balance. Again the paper was spread: "Eight Protestants. Nine Catholics." Providence could be counted on, eventually. The following morning young Bertie, sent perhaps on a distant errand, might stray from his own Protestant section of Ballymacarrett into a Catholic area and hear history in "the flip of a skipping-rope, and the street-rhyme that went with it":

> Holy Father, what'll I do.
> I've come to confess my sins to you.
> Holy Father, I killed a cat.
> You'll have to suffer, my child, for that.
> Holy Father, what'll it be?
> Forty days without any tea.
> Father dear, it's far too long.
> You've done, my child, a very great wrong.
> But Father dear, 'twas a Protestant cat.
> Good, my girl, you did right to do that.

Both of Rodgers's parents were from County Down families, Jane Ferris McCarey from Dundonald, just

east of Belfast, and Robert Skelly Rodgers from
Dromara, farther south below Ballynahinch. Both
families were thoroughly Scots Presbyterian in origin,
but the McCareys had been in Ireland longer, probably
since Cromwell's day. Robert Skelly Rodgers had been
married before but widowed. He worked for a large
Belfast insurance company and earned enough and
was thrifty enough to provide a modest but adequate
and—most important for Jane Ferris McCarey Rodgers
—respectable house, facing onto a decent street of other
houses and shops. But "wee barefoot fellows" lived in
the low-down streets at the back.

Rodgers left us two or three glimpses of his childhood, most notably and delightfully in his B.B.C. radio
play, *The Return Room*, from which the above quota-
tions have been taken, and in a little book of prose
reflections, *Essex Roundabout*. The play is a sound-
portrait of daily life in the house at Mountpottinger
Corner, above the River Lagan valley, the shining cur-
rent sluicing through it "fluted like a stick of celery."
Belfast, for all its ships and mills and factories, was
still a countryman's city in those days. "Cocks crowed
in the back-yards, and cattle straggled the streets on
their way to the docks. A blacksmith's anvil chirped
like a grasshopper in the cobbled lane beside us . . ."
The ordinary sights and sounds and smells of the city
touched the lyrical heart of the child and, later, the
lyrical pen of the poet—the "carts dripping with wet
slummage from the distillery," the "little shops with
string dangling from coloured cannisters," the terse
rhythmic talk of family and neighbors. "I would give,"
he wrote, "a sugar-bag of polite talk for just one nip

of their bitter old puritan tongues, one pull of their
racy old pipes," and he meant it.

Kites, kali-suckers, comics, cigarettes, and such "pagan
surprises" as following the May queen, with her dress
of old lace-curtains and her wreath of paper flowers—
there were all these along their road. But his puritan
mother was there, too, saying, "It would suit you better
to be thinking of your latter-end."

> Life at best is very brief,
> Like the falling of a leaf,
> Like the binding of a sheaf,
> Be in time . . .

And in bed at night, the boy could hear his father,
his voice rising and falling like the wind on the roof,
reading aloud from the Book: ". . . as for man his days
are as grass: as a flower of the field so he flourisheth.
For the wind passeth over it and it is gone . . ." Always
the warnings against life's vanities, always the call to
think on death. There were no full-length mirrors in
that house, lest one get too enamoured of oneself. And
not a drop of liquor. Even Shakespeare was forbidden.
After a great row and soul-searching, young Bertie
was permitted to see a school production because of
his interest in literature; but his twin sister, Reah,
had to stay home.

Sundays were worst of all. Sunday is the day when
the children's swings are chained shut in Belfast parks.
"Sunday dinner was cooked on Saturday, and the Sunday boots were polished the night before, and profane
books and music were put away till Monday, and
nothing, absolutely nothing, was allowed to disturb

'the Day of Dreadful Rest' as we restless children called
it." The city with the "red-brick face" doffed its
"factory-hat of smoke" and the houses "looked as if
they had gone round the corner on Saturday night
and come back with their faces coffined . . . There was
a horrible smell of goodness everywhere, in my navy-
blue suit, in my celluloid collar, in my shiny new boots
that squeaked as I walked." His mother, being so
respectable that, were you running for your life, she
would have had you stop to tie your laces, liked the
squeak in the boots. As a girl she had had her boots
made specially squeaky, so the whole church could
hear their respectability.

In July each year the family would move to a holiday cottage outside Belfast. One can easily forget,
amid the sooty gloom of that city, that its puritan
center is ringed by a halo of mountains and that
heather and streams and game are but half an hour
away. "The duck twirled like a stick on the stream,
each gay cloud was off on its own, the very clod sang.
Apart from my enemy, the nettle, there was only one
flaw to it all." And that was the gospel tents, descending "on our fields like pentecostal tongues, and the
reapers of souls cut great swathes of hymns through
the standing silence." Now the boy longed to be back
in Belfast for the Twelfth of July, "to hear the dreadful
thunder of the big Orange drums" celebrating King
William III's crossing of the Boyne in 1690. Or at
least to be left alone to celebrate the green summer
days. He watched with "fascinated horror" the pig
killing, the blowing up of bladders like balloons, and
the drinking of "salubrious draughts" of the pig's blood.

"There's good health in it, boy: great health, if only you knowed it." But the gospel songs reminded him of the blood of the Lamb. "Mystery, all of it. So much redness to redeem all this greenness. So much death to make life everlasting. The big red drum that sounded every day across the fields seemed to repeat the dark refrain. But the gay little fife that went with it spoke of life."

One might easily get from *The Return Room* an idea of Bertie Rodgers as a boy just waiting for his chance to wriggle out of his navy-blue suit and his celluloid collar and skip to the natural world, to freedom, even, God save him, to Dublin. Surely he lingers most lovingly on secular things and portrays his religion and goodness and respectability as heavy hands pushed over his eyes. Pulled away by his mother from a game of rounders to a gospel meeting, he "felt the bitterness of the world. I knew now why a fellow might go and get himself into jail just to escape from so much goodness."

But Bertie Rodgers was not a boy to go to jail. He heard the call of the fife and his heart may have raced to it, but he was timid, shy and afraid, and he liked the beat of the big red drum of death, too. He needed to hear the two together. This was a boy so shy that in all his years at school he had his sister Reah pay his ten shilling coal fees for him, so he would not have to face the teacher. So shy that if he had a new coat, he would have Reah and his younger sister, Jean, step out into the road before him, to make sure no one they knew was in sight. He was not about to shun safe harbor. He was snug, or so he then felt, in the con-

traries of this Belfast life and death. "Gay goes up and
grim comes down. The Puritan pepper and salt, if it
looked like granite tasted like drama. It had two sides
to it. Everything in Belfast had two sides." Wiser, so
he thought, not to choose between sides but to seek
delight and equilibrium from their clashes.

> Few are thy days and full of woe,
> O man of woman born!
> Thy doom is written, "Dust thou art,
> And shalt to dust return!"
>
> Cheered by this hope, with patient mind
> I'll wait heaven's high decree,
> Till the appointed period come
> When death shall set us free. Amen.

So he waited, and passed through his Belfast boy-
hood and young manhood, doing excellent work in
school, entering Queen's University, where he devel-
oped a liking for Wordsworth and Tennyson, and receiving his B.A. with honors in English literature in
1931. But what to do now?

He hesitated. His father wanted him to start work.
Instead, he entered the Presbyterian Theological College to prepare for the ministry and, on January 25,
1935, was ordained.

> Life at best is very brief,
> Like the falling of a leaf,
> Like the binding of a sheaf,
> Be in time . . .

2
Paired Lives

Rodgers looked upon joining the ministry as a way of not having to choose a career. He thought of it chiefly as a means of being left alone to be or to become himself. He feared having a job with regular hours and a boss giving him orders. Sound enough fears, but he had not calculated the special pressures on a parson, nor could he forsee how these and certain pressures in his personal life would drive him away from his ministry and into poetry and other arms.

Not that he lacked faith. At the time of his ordination, if he had any religious doubts they were of the manageable sort which can coexist with faith and even strengthen it. He was already in love with contraries. He was able to accept his doubts in the same way that he could accept and delight in the Saturday–Sunday oppositions of his childhood. Twenty years after his ordination he would write, "Maybe it is the liking for strong black and white contrast that makes me partial to the Belfast I knew, with its long files of women and girls in black shawls, streaming out of the linen mills;

or the dark city at dusk with the rain stippling the puddles and silvering the pavements, and the 'Island-men' thronging the red tramcars and filling the red-blinded pubs. What drink then could be more proper than the white-headed pints of black porter? It was in Belfast too that I came across a dark and curious usage among house-painters. There I have seen them mix a bottle of stout into the paint in the belief that it fixed the colour better and gave it a lasting quality." Let doubt then be the stout to his faith. And I suppose this is the place to mention that the young minister did take a drink—though not, to be sure, in public—at a time when Presbyterian ministers were not supposed to drink at all. In 1969, after Rodgers's death, I over-heard a distant relation of his, muttering, "What black mischief was hiding behind that white collar!"

His choice of a wife seems to have been a part of this scheme of oppositions. He had met Marie Harden Waddell when she and he were students at Queen's. Then, while he was preparing for the ministry and she was completing her medical studies, Rodgers suffered an accident which brought them together again. Rodgers had been knocked off his motor-bike while riding in the country outside Belfast. The motorist, evidently in a state of panic, reversed over Rodgers's chest as he lay in the road. He sustained several broken ribs and bled from the mouth, and Marie Harden Wad-dell helped to attend to him at the hospital. Intelligent, proud, quick-witted, sharp-tongued, Marie Harden Waddell had a vigorous, nervous beauty which altogether fascinated Rodgers. Her physical and intel-lectual vitality seemed complementary to his diffident

and rather dreamy nature. If she was religiously ir-
reverent and even frankly dubious about Rodgers's
profession, that was all the livelier and all the better,
another bottle of stout in the paint. With her, he might
learn to be more at home in the world. With him, her
bright rationalism might soften under his lyrical sense
of the mystery of things. A year after his ordination, he
brought her to his parish at Loughgall, County Armagh.
She was to be the village physician. While he was
ministering to the souls of his flock, she would look
after their bodies.

Loughgall lies about 35 miles southeast of Belfast
amid the green hills and fruit orchards between Porta-
down and Armagh City. It is a hidden place, and if
you are coming from Belfast to search it out, you must
sneak up on it slowly and gently, circling away from and
just south of it on the small old roads. Finally you are
heading north and seemingly wrong, when the road
runs up the hump of a hill, and you are beside the
church and in Loughgall.

Cloveneden Church, from which Rodgers ministered
for twelve years to a hundred families, was built in
1712—small, simple, and beautiful in its rectangular
proportions. Its stuccoed walls are a pale apple-green;
inside it is spare, clean and light, and the original
yellow-brown wooden pews remain to this day. From
the hilltop churchyard the country dips and rises and
rolls out gently in an Irish-English way, the fields green
enough to make your eyes ache, the orderly orchards
telling of the Ulsterman's patience and industry. Or as
Rodgers put it (in his *Ireland in Colour*): "Armagh
with its orchards, outlined with delicate white plum

blossom in April, and bosomed with pink apple blossom in May, bespeaks an English settlement, but its lime-washed eighteenth-century farmhouses, ochre and pink, and salmon, have the Irish habit."

The minister's manse was one of these Georgian farmhouses, spacious and stately, with its own apple orchard and field. But the minister's stipend being about £250 per year, the field was let out for another £10 yearly. To this was added Marie's small earnings as doctor to the hundred Loughgall families. There was another doctor in the village, but his practice shrank as Marie's grew, for her intelligence and quickness at diagnosis was quickly appreciated, and the idea of seeing the doctor in the minister's own house must have appealed to the sick and pious.

It was in Loughgall, in the fourth year of his ministry, that Rodgers finally discovered the poet in himself. His parents had always sensed something extraordinary (although that word would not have been in their cautious Northern vocabulary) in him, and when several of his essays won medals at Queen's, they might have suspected that his talent lay in writing. But he had never so much as written a poem, and if he had, his practical-minded parents would not have especially welcomed it. When he did publish his first book in 1940, at the age of 31, his father's only comment was, "I wouldn't tell anybody. They'll think you are wasting your time."

What made him write? His attachment to the land, for one thing, an attachment so strong that it had to find expression. It was Rodgers's way to give himself over totally, physically and spiritually, to the landscapes of his life—Belfast, Loughgall, and, later, parts of England and even California. But Loughgall and what lay just beyond it, Armagh City and the Mourne Mountains to the southeast, more than any other places seeped in through his senses, got turned into words and became

IRELAND

O these lakes and all gills that live in them,
These acres and all legs that walk on them,
These tall winds and all wings that cling to them,
Are part and parcel of me, bit and bundle,
Thumb and thimble. Them I am . . .

His theme here may be similar to but is less historical than Yeats's in "To Ireland in the Coming Times" or "I am of Ireland." By speaking of himself, the poet, as a being so connected with nature as to have become one with it, Rodgers invites the criticism that he has reached behind Yeats to write warmed-over Wordsworth. Bring on a leech-gatherer strangely metamorphosing himself into rock and shadow and cloud, allude to Coleridge on the primary imagination, and the idea vanishes into early Romantic mist. But Rodgers was not trading in shopworn conventions, nor was he faking the emotions and beliefs which form his theme. When we consider his background and the nature of the tiny rural society to which he was minister, we can expect a few hoary-headed ideas. His talent, first, and the intensity and authenticity of his feelings, second, matter more. Consider the language of—

STORMY DAY

O look how the loops and balloons of bloom
Bobbing on long strings from the finger-ends

> And knuckles of the lurching cherry-tree
> Heap and hug, elbow and part, this wild day,
> Like a careless carillon cavorting;
> And the beaded whips of the beeches splay
> And dip like anchored weed round a drowned rock,
> And hovering effortlessly the rooks
> Hang on the wind's effrontery as if
> On hooks, then loose their hold and slide away
> Like sleet sidewards down the warm swimming sweep
> Of wind. O it is a lovely time . . .

This much of that poem is pure celebration of the simple play of wind and trees and birds; and the language and rhythm, inspired in part at least by Hopkins, not only convey the scene to us with astonishing vividness, they also convince us of the speaker's union with the subject matter. We sense no middleman here between us and the tossing trees. The poet does seem part and parcel, bit and bundle of a stormy day.

In a few instances Rodgers was content to describe a scene and to imply his emotional reaction to it.

> Of the Mournes I remember most the mist,
> The grey granite goosefleshed, the minute
> And blazing parachutes of fuchsia, and us
> Listening to the tiny clustered slinks
> Of little chisels tinkling tirelessly
> On stone, like a drip of birds' beaks picking
> Rapidly at scattered grain. . . .

The surprising imagery, the yoking of sounds related if not rhyming, the half-suggested onomatopoeia, the alliteration—all characteristic and effective, though occasionally, especially the alliteration, overdone.

But usually, somewhere in each poem, Rodgers tries to go beyond description to make a point or to point a moral. The stormy day is marred by news-posters

announcing war, the memory of lively places leadens
to a lump in the mind. Sometimes the message—that
is just what it is—slips in unobtrusively and gracefully
and the poem glides successfully to its close. But too
often, in this early work, the moral gets poked through
on the end of a wagging finger, and one feels preached
at. The preacher turned poet has not yet discovered how
to get down from his pulpit. The most obvious instances of this confusion of poetry with sermonizing
involve Rodgers's unfortunate predeliction for person-
ification. I suspect that only a special kind of satire
could permit such characters as Humbug, Rut and
Rout, Butt and Rebut, Bother, Goodness, Evil, Vio-
lence, Reason and Faith to survive on the stage of
twentieth-century poetry. Wordsworth, perhaps; Bun-
yan, probably not. Rodgers may have been inspired by
Hopkins's sounds and rhythms but not often enough
by that other preacher-poet's indirect method of statement.

He seems to have regarded the writing of his poetry
in a Pentecostal way—as a visitation of words which
gave the poet his gift of expression, the poet being a
passive recipient:

WORDS

Always the arriving winds of words
Pour like the Atlantic gales over these ears,
These reefs, these foils and fenders, these shrinking
And sea-scalded edges of the brain-land.
Rebutted and rebounding, on they post
Past my remembrance, falling all unplanned.
But some day out of darkness they'll come forth,
Arrowed and narrowed into my tongue's tip,
And speak for me—their most astonished host.

This conception derives from the Christian definition
of priest or minister as God's instrument and ultimately
from the idea of the apostles having had the gift of
tongues by virtue of the visitation of the Holy Spirit.
Many poets have held to this view of themselves, but
in Rodgers's case I think it is another indication of his
initial failure to distinguish sufficiently between the
poet and the parson in himself.

The moralizing tone of some of these poems and the
wholly personal tone of others suggest the psychological
and moral confusions under which Rodgers was beginning to labor. Lover of contraries though he was,
the vise of his professional and personal conflicts proved
excruciating. He had thought that the ministry and
Loughgall itself would be refuges for him to think his
thoughts and walk the hills and watch his children
grow. But inevitably he became involved in what he
called, in a late, unpublished essay, "the subtle tensions
of an old and balanced community . . ." Not only was
he required to enter into these tensions; he, as the
minister, was regarded as the final arbiter and spiritual
authority in what, no matter the kind of government
ruling from London or Belfast or Dublin, was essen-
tially a miniature theocracy. "A rural community is a
close and intricate wickerwork of human relationships
and functions. Each person born into it, or brought
into it, is given a pertinent rôle to fill and is always
identified with this rôle. The rôle I was called to fill
was that of parson and, being young, I found it a
formidable one. Old men, full of worldly experience,
farmers who never hesitated to advise me on practical
matters, would at once defer to me, as sons to a father,

when it came to other-worldly matters and spiritual crises. Not that they were impressed by my personal authority; authority for them resided in the rôle and office which I happened to occupy . . . I realised that I, as an individual, did not matter, and this in a way was a relief to me as well as an instruction. I do not know how one would carry the problems of a community if one were only oneself. The danger, of course— and this goes for all men who fill a public rôle and wear a public mask, parson or politician—the danger is that a man may end by confusing the office with himself. If this happens he becomes simply a mask, an empty shell, a private bore in public and a public bore in private."

Rodgers was in fact a most effective and beloved parson. Even today his ministry is remembered with affection by the people of Loughgall, and his photograph hangs in the vestibule of Cloveneden Church. He certainly looked the part—a parsonish pallor in his face, his hair dark, his eyes an impenetrable dark diffusing brown, yet paradoxically intent. He moved with a slow, careful, gentle dignity and grace. His sermons were exceptional literary as well as spiritual experiences for the congregation. He spoke as he always did, publicly and privately, in a haunting, mystical manner, hovering over individual words, his accent softer than the typical Northerner's, his voice rather soft too, with a portentous air about it, hinting of things unseen. He used to reserve a portion of each sermon for the children. He would speak to them simply, directly and gently, with reassurances rather than damnations, and the entire congregation enjoyed this practice best. He was also effective in dealing with the personal problems of his parishioners. "I can cross the counters," he often said of himself, a horse-racing expression meaning the ability to see both sides of a dispute. In a parish where the Orange Order was founded and where passions were quick to rise, he became known as "the Catholic Presbyterian."

Yet his successes gave him little comfort. And as some of his early poetry attests, he had indeed begun "to confuse the office with himself." Every clergyman must occasionally feel uncomfortable playing the part of God's anointed. Rodgers sensed that he had assumed the role without first discovering his identity and began to doubt that he ever could discover it while still in costume. Alone in his study at the manse, he castigated himself in verse:

TO THE PREACHER

You suck in Good,
And spit out Sin
Just as you would
A spent grape-skin.

Light as a glove
You separate
The thing you love
From that you hate.

But this divorce
And glib conclusion
Is got, of course,
By their collusion.

Then too, the world beyond Loughgall started to attract him. The approaching war drew his mind across

seas he had not thought of crossing. And as he fashioned
his verses, the poetry of other men of his generation
began to fascinate him. A friend from his university
days, John Hewitt, himself a skillful poet, introduced
him to the work of Auden, Spender, Day Lewis, and
another Belfastman, Louis MacNeice. Loughgall, small
and ordered, "rounded as the belly of a pebble you
would pick up on the seashore," pinched. "I had grown
too much into the communal world and it had become
static for me. It was always afternoon in my parish, the
full tide of sleep brimming the sky; the shot bird hung
in the air, the blown rose refused to fall, the clock stood
still." By 1940, even the war itself seemed preferable
to this pastoral stasis:

> . . . You will be more free
> At the thoughtless centre of slaughter than you would be
> Standing chained to the telephone-end while the world
>   cracks.

It may be, however, that the burdens of his profession
would not have weighed so heavily upon him had his
marriage not become the heaviest burden of all. Here
again, the clashes and contraries he had relished battered him into thoughts of escape. Marie's skepticism
about the value of the ministry only deepened his own
doubts and, as one would suspect, enabled him to trans-
late some of those doubts into resentment against her.
If he was fed up, well then, Marie would taunt, let him
do something about it. But Rodgers was as passive as
she was active. He was not ready to go further than the
writing of poems to find a way out. He thought of
himself, Romantically and Calvinistically, as a kind of

Aeolian harp, upon which the winds of fate would play. Such aimlessness was thoroughly exasperating to a strong-willed woman like Marie. Rodgers wrote about their daily life:

THE LOVERS

After the tiff there was stiff silence, till
One word, flung in centre like a single stone,
Starred and cracked the ice of her resentment
To its edge. From that stung core opened and
Poured up one outward and widening wave
Of eager and extravagant anger.

A fine and frightening poem. What was the tiff about? What was the one word that cracked open the core? No matter. The anger, hysterical anger, is made all the more powerful by our not knowing its specific cause.

And the truth is that Rodgers did not know its cause. Oh there were the obvious ones—his growing melancholy and feeling of uselessness; the simple fact that their life together had gradually turned into a battle of oppositions and not the union of opposites he had anticipated; the sad knowledge that the birth of children was not making a difference, was only more cause for conflict. A son had been stillborn; a daughter, Harden, was born in 1939 and another, Nini, in 1941. Three "aunts," actually cousins of Marie's father, had come to live in the manse and help care for the children. But their presence, rather than making it possible for husband and wife to come closer together, only freed Marie to brood and anguish.

Her practice, as I indicated above, had prospered in Loughgall, but her health had not prospered with it.

Increasingly, she became subject to fits of anxiety, depression, and hysteria. Scenes like the one described in "The Lovers" became commonplace. She looked to Rodgers for the strength which the mentally distraught so often try to borrow from someone else, and when he could not provide it, she overwhelmed him with her "eager and extravagant anger." Rodgers, moreover, was not the sort of person who gave strong direction or advice to anyone—one of the reasons for his feeling ill-cast in his parson's role. He existed, he stayed afloat, awash with his contradictions. There was example in that, but not what Marie wanted. Uselessly she prodded and clawed at him. At times the situation came close to displaying itself in public—not a happy circumstance for a pair so publicly important in the community. Marie's patients would be waiting to see her. Behind her office door, she and Rodgers quarrelled violently, until Marie's anger poured over the low wall bordering hysteria. She would be screaming and smashing things, with Parson Rodgers running back and forth, trying to calm her down one moment and the next assuring her patients that she would look after them shortly.

Each became the other's best enemy and, to retreat, they drank, so their rows became drunken ones. They preserved the outward forms, but as time passed only their hostile connections remained vital. Rodgers summed it up in one superbly precise and depressing poem:

PAIRED LIVES

Though to stranger's approach
(Like swing doors cheek to cheek)

Presenting one smooth front
Of summed resistance and
Aligned resentment, yet
On nearer view note how,
At the deflecting touch
Of intervening hand
Each in its lonely arc
Reaches and rocks inward
(Retires and returns
Immediately to join
The other moiety).
Each singly yields to thrust,
Is hung on its own hinge
Of fear and hope, and in
Its own reticence rests.

Is there an apter hymn to married love?

The frequency of Marie's attacks of hysteria increased, and in order to ward them off, she became dependent on morphine, available to her as a doctor.

Often the parson himself would be sent to fetch it. The personality conflicts, the drinking, and the hysteria produced an intolerable situation—yet Rodgers tolerated it, whether out of weakness, indecision, forbearance, resignation, who can say?

Poetry, together with his involvement in the life of the community, gave him some solace, though the latter, as we have seen, threatened to usurp his individual identity. He felt hounded—literally. One of his superb poems describes the poet's identification with a frightened hare chased by hounds:

BEAGLES

Over rock and wrinkled ground
Ran the lingering nose of hound

The little and elastic hare
Stretched herself nor stayed to stare;

Stretched herself and far away
Darted through the chinks of day,
Behind her shouting out her name
The whole blind world hilarious came.

Over hills a running line
Curled like a whiplash, fast and fine,
Past me sailed the sudden pack
Along the taut and tingling track.

From the far flat scene each shout
Like jig-saw piece came tumbling out
I took and put them all together
And then they turned into a tether,
A tether that held me to the hare
Here there and everywhere.

The excellence of this poem—indeed its only flaw is its
off-target title—seems self-evident. If we are thinking
of Rodgers's life, it conveys the breathless fear he must
have felt at that time. He became so fascinated by this
form of hunt, because of what it implied of life, that
for years he purchased and collected every item of talk
and information about the hare that he could. "My
heart was with the hare, quick and elusive, and yet
the loud spectacle of the running hounds wakened some
old complicity in the blood." He discovered that some
of the local hounds were named after the Greek furies
—Megaera was one. He found that practically every
farmer owned a hound and that the hunt was the only
social activity in which both Catholic and Protestant
participated. Although the purpose of the hunt was
the death of the hare, cares were taken to facilitate her
escape, so that she might give another good run some

other day. No one, not even in times of rationing, would shoot a hare. And it was the common belief that the hare ran always in a circle. Years after leaving Loughgall, he dramatized the hunt and its lore in a radio script (*The Hare,* never produced) and, in 1963, he summed up his findings and his conclusions in a chapter of his *Essex Roundabout* called "The full circle": "I could see now the unconscious logic of it all. What I was looking at was not just a sport but an age-old folk play about life and death . . . a play of opposites in which the antagonists were hare and hound, the stage was the countryside, and the chorus the huntsmen. And why, in this play, had the country-folk with unconscious accuracy cast the hare in the rôle of life? Because of her cunning, her ability to outwit death. . . .

"In the long run, of course, death will overtake her, and will run her down. But meanwhile let her have a clear warning, a fair run, and a square deal. And let no meddling hand, no mercenary gun, anticipate her end. For this play of hare and hound bodies forth man's feeling about his own predicament, his mortal condition. He himself is the hunted one who has the rendezvous with death.

"And why should the play be enacted on a revolving stage? Why does the hare run in a circle? Because, says country lore, her course is a paradigm of man's earthly course.

> For as the hare whom hounds and horn pursue
> Pants to the place from which at first she flew

so man too returns to the place from whence he came forth. In his beginning is his end."

How could Rodgers at least go through the ritual of running until at last run down? From time to time he would write poems celebrating his old virtues, clash and conflict, the liberating stimuli of oppositions, himself feeling trapped and worn down by those very things. "Directions to a Rebel," one of his best-known pieces, advises the welcoming of strife, malice, enmity: "these things/Will shape and sharp your purpose, stroke and strop/Your temper, point your passionate aim." Brendan Behan told Rodgers that an Irishman in Parkhurst Gaol was sure the poem had been written for the I.R.A. and had pinned it up on the prison wall. Yet Rodgers's own rebellion remained confined to words. Hounded, feeling run down at last, he was

THE INTERNED REFUGEE

And I was left here in the darkened house,
Listening for the fat click of the softly-shut door,
Looking for the oiled glint and ghost of light
Sliding soundlessly along the wall toward me,
Knowing that round me They were mobilising
Their cold implacable forces slowly.

I shouted and none answered, one by one
My listening hopes crept back to me
Out of that dead place; mine was a lighted face
Looking into darkness, seen, but seeing nothing.

Sketch of a mental landscape.

3
The Fall

The publication of *Awake! And other poems* by Secker & Warburg in 1940 let in some light. The first printing was destroyed by the blitz on Plymouth—one can imagine Rodgers's reaction—but the publishers brought out a second printing in 1941. An American edition (Harcourt, Brace) appeared in 1942. The book contained all the poems Rodgers had written up to 1940—and the first had been written in 1938. Reviews were many and very favorable, though with reservations about Rodgers's "unrestrained verbosity," in Stephen Spender's unrestrained phrase. James Stephens informed Rodgers that he had read the book with delight and had written comments on every page; Stephens's nephew copied out the comments for Rodgers, who cherished them for the rest of his life. It was Rodgers's lyricism, the freshness and joy of some of the nature poems, the dancing cadences, which appealed most to a public already grey and weary of war and the poetry of ashes. "Suddenly all the fountains in the park/Opened smoothly their umbrellas of water." That was life-giving reading while bombs were falling.

His own familiar reading now included the Irish sagas, Yeats, Joyce, Synge, Gogarty, and the strong young voices from the South, O'Flaherty, O'Connor, O'Faolain. Away in his tiny vest-pocket of the North, he could know little of Dublin literary life, yet the more he read and wrote the more he began to feel brother of the company that sang to sweeten Ireland and to vex her. North and South became one to him; as he put it, "I had a foot in both graves." He sensed, accurately, that Dublin, though a provincial capital, must be a more cosmopolitan place than any he had known. And the easyness of Southern life, with its tolerance of extremes and its ceaseless flow of the best talk in all the world, beckoned him. Feeling that his personal world was splitting up, feeling war within and without himself, he was looking for a way out and for a "newfoundland," a place, as he wrote of it at the time,

NEITHER HERE NOR THERE

In that land all is, and nothing's ought;
No owners or notices, only birds;
No walls anywhere, only lean wire of words
Worming brokenly out from eaten thought;
No oats growing, only ankle-lace grass
Easing not resenting the feet that pass . . .
No contracts, entails, hereditaments,
Anything that might tie or hem.
In that land all's lackadaisical . . .
On clear days mountains of meaning are seen
Humped high on the horizon; no one goes
To con their meaning, no one cares or knows. . . .

No Cause there comes to term, but each departs
Elsewhere to whelp its deeds, expel its darts;
There are no homecomings, no good-byes
In that land, neither yearning nor scorning,
Though at night there is the smell of morning.

The unstated yearning for death is obvious enough in
that poem, but to Rodgers at the time almost any place
out of the North seemed to fit the description, and the
South seemed to fit it especially well.

Rodgers could not bring himself to depart Loughgall
forever but, in the summer of 1941, he decided on a
two- or three-week holiday in Dublin, by himself. On
the train he felt oddly unreal, as though it were the
Orient Express, and at the border, when asked for his
identity card (it was wartime and he was entering a
neutral country), he wondered who he was, anyway.
He had written no one in Dublin of his coming. But
Geoffrey Taylor, editor of *The Bell*, had included a
favorable review of *Awake!* in his magazine; and when
Rodgers knocked on the door of his country house at
Tallaght, just southwest of Dublin, Taylor welcomed
him, and he stayed there for days and days.

It was a new, un-Northern world: paintings on the
walls, shelves and shelves of poetry. "In the North,"
Rodgers recalled years later, "one had always half-
apologised for poetry. . . . Here in this Dublin house
poetry was plainly accepted as a sensible normal public
preoccupation, a logical way of life, a progress. A great
relief from the arithmetical progress of the North. Geoffrey Taylor would have given me any book of prose
from his large library, but never a book of verse. For
Verse was a necessity, not a frill or a foible." He and
Taylor talked about poetry at all hours, and Rodgers

marvelled at Taylor's spirited knowledge. "He was one of three who knew the corpus of English poetry so well that he could cull and recall the one solitary bright line from an otherwise endlessly dull and mediocre poet; he delighted to do this." Taylor took Rodgers on rounds of literary friends—Austin Clarke, Frank O'Connor, John Betjeman, Sean O'Sullivan. How the parson relished all that literary gossip—"the lashings and leavings and lovings of good talk about writers and writing that was my first visit to Dublin." And the lashings of drink.

One day Taylor placed in Rodgers's hands R. A. S. Macalister's *Ancient Ireland*. Rodgers was particularly struck by Macalister's description of the famous monastery of Tallaght and its heretical monks who remained there defying the rule of Rome into the ninth century. Their "solitary survival" appealed to him, made him think of himself, and brought to his mind the image of a single and solitary bird. There at Tallaght, he fashioned the poem which was to remain his personal favorite, "The Swan," which concludes,

> On that grey lake, frilled round with scufflings
> Of foam and milled with muttering,
> I saw lingering, late and lightless,
> A single swan, swinging, sleek as a sequin.
>
> Negligently bright, wide wings pinned back,
> It mooned on the moving water,
> And not all the close and gathering dark
> Or gathering wind could lift or flatter
> That small and dimming image into flight;
> Far from shore and free from foresight,
> Coiled in its own indifferent mood
> It held the heavens, shores, waters and
>   all their brood.

Looking ahead to his return to Loughgall, he hoped to
survive solitary as the swan, holding the brood of all
his thoughts within the elegance and grace of his poems.

If his contact with men like Taylor had given him a
new sense of the importance and vitality of poetry, it
had also introduced him to the companionship of men
more like himself than any he had known, and, back at
Loughgall, he thought of himself again as the interned
refugee—this time a refugee from an Irish heaven of
convivial poets. He thought of O'Faolain's translation
of the ancient Irish monk's "Heavenly Banquet":

> I should like to have the men of heaven
> In my own house
> With vats of good cheer
> Laid out for them.
>
> I should like a great lake of beer
> For the King of Kings
> I should like to see heaven's company
> Drinking it through all eternity.

Yet in his own house and out in the parish the same
sorrows bedeviled him. He kept on for another year or
so, struggling with flock and family, turning to poetry
for ease and insight.

Marie's illness finally forced Rodgers into at least a
partial decision. She needed psychiatric treatment, and
that meant getting out of Loughgall for a time. Through
friends they had heard of a Jungian analyst in Oxford
whose ideas and reputation appealed to Marie. Rodgers
took a year's leave of absence from his parish and, in
the summer of 1943, departed with Marie for Oxford.
The two girls were left behind in the care of the aunts.

One wonders what hopes Rodgers had for the success of this plan, but certainly he was glad to get away from Loughgall, and since he knew he would return, he could be free of guilt about abandoning his responsibilities there. The life of Oxford, not just the intellectual but the pub-life as well, naturally agreed with him. Yet it was an exceedingly difficult year.

For one thing, Marie's illness was quite as serious as one expected: the diagnosis was schizophrenia. There was hope of the effectiveness of analysis, and Marie began to think of going on to become a psychoanalyst herself, but her prospects were doubtful. Rodgers, moreover, was at a loss away from all familiar things. "Split world, split feeling, split land, split loyalties, split smile"—he knew less now than ever who he was or where he was going, and the absence of his pastoral duties only increased his sense of uselessness. Talk and drink became and were to remain his dearest pleasures, and he achieved a reputation for greatness in both realms, but neither could relieve his sense of purposelessness. Marie's analysis made him think of his own mind in a way detached from traditional Irish and Biblical modes, and he began to worry about his psychological state. For about four months he visited a psychoanalyst. He recorded his dreams, illustrating them with pictures and diagrams of the action. Some of his dreambooks have survived. I do not know how he or his analyst interpreted them, but they add psychological perspective to our understanding of the conflicts within his personality and poetry.

One situation recurs frequently. He stands before his congregation, unable to speak for one reason or another.

Either he has lost his voice or, more often, has forgotten to prepare his sermon. Here are his conscious and unconscious fears about his professional role, as well as his desires for these fears and confusions to be made public. In two such dreams a conflict breaks out in the church. People are screaming at each other, and huge guns fire long blue flames.

The guns suggest a connection between fears of professional and sexual inadequacy—but most of the dreams are far more explicit in their sexual content. He has finished his sermon but is unsure of its effect and feels great tensions. A young girl of the parish greets him at the top of a flight of stairs in the church and kisses him. He is grateful but alarmed. She leads him down the stairs, he feels he should not go with her, but he leans over and kisses her. They stand beside a door which suddenly opens. Inside his mother sits, sewing. The girl, embarrassed, runs away. His mother offers him new clerical garments which she has been preparing for him. But he sees that they are decorated in bright red, and he fears that they are quite inappropriate. He compromises by wearing the red-decorated coat but keeping his plain black trousers.

Certain elements seem accessible enough and require no detailed psychoanalytic interpretation. He feels a conflict between his parson's role and his natural instincts, clearly sexual here. He yields to the instincts while fearing them—kissing the girl and descending the stairs with her—but then he is confronted with the conscience-figure of his puritan mother. Further anxieties arise because of the garish clothes she sews for him. Is she, of all people, tempting him? The "compromise" with which the dream ends only emphasizes his confusions.

In a similar dream, he is sitting next to a girl at a prayer meeting. The girl offers him cigarettes. He replies, with some embarrassment, thinking it out of place to smoke at such a meeting, "No, thank you. I *have* some cigarettes." Then, "to slur over the refusal, I jokingly asked her why she didn't offer one to John on my right (everyone knew he didn't smoke, on principle.) " John stands up and gives testimony. Then Rodgers gives his testimony. As a boy of fourteen or fifteen, he says, he came under a deep conviction of sin and the need for salvation. He saw that the wages of sin is death.

The dream hints at several aspects of Rodgers's guilts and confusions. He feels he must refuse the cigarettes because his public conscience, or, if you like, his superego, tells him that they are wrong. Yet he is embarrassed by his refusal and doesn't want the girl to think him less than a man. The girl probably represents Marie. The "slurring over" of his refusal by referring to the abstemious John is probably his way of trying to say to the girl, or to Marie, "Well, after all, there are some men even worse (or more inadequate) than I." But in the end he joins John in a public renunciation of "sin." Here the dreamer probably expresses the wish that his guilts and fears could be resolved just as they had been when he was a boy. The reappearance of his mother would not have been out of place at this point.

Many of the dreams increase one's understanding of the conflict between Rodgers and Marie. I shall cite three examples.

Rodgers and Marie are out walking in the woods. He spies a "pine-tree bird"—instead of feathers, the bird is covered with stiff pine-needles. He calls to Marie to look at it, she refuses. "You're so apathetic," he says to her. So she does look—but only into an empty meadow. This annoys and enrages Rodgers.

If we can accept certain basic psychoanalytic symbol-values, the woods represent feminine material, the bird with its stiff needles phallic material, the meadow again female material. Thus the dream conveys Rodgers's feelings of sexual inadequacy towards Marie. He suffers from her indifference, and when she does respond, she sees not a sign of masculinity but a symbol of the female genitalia. The dream shows that Rodgers doubted his sexual identity as much as his professional one. Hence his annoyance and anger at what Marie sees—whether she is merely accusing him or actually discovering something.

In another dream, he meets Marie in the office of the commandant of a Nazi prison camp. He is obsequious to the commandant and tries to convert him to the benign teachings of Christ. The commandant remains unmoved. Outside, Marie berates him and mocks him for his parsonish performance, calling him a fool. (At this point one discerns an allegory of Rodgers's marriage as a kind of prison camp, with Rodgers unsure of his masculine role and Marie identified with the oppressors.) He goes into the Hotel Metropole and comes out carrying a bucket of water. This ending seems ambiguous to me: Rodgers, as the dreamer, is fulfilling a wish either to appropriate the female role for himself or to gain control over, to possess the female, neither of which he seems able to do in life.

In the most elaborate and fascinating of all his recorded dreams, Rodgers sees himself walking with a boy
to the May Fair. They come to a wall, which the boy
hops over easily; but Rodgers must struggle, as he is
carrying some sort of heavy and cumbersome burden.
They arrive at the Fair and pause before a display of
pipes, many of them with strangely-shaped bowls. They
examine several of the pipes, peering down into the
bowls, deliberating whether to buy one. Suddenly the
boy goes off to enjoy himself "wildly." Rodgers enters
a café where several of his friends have gathered. One
of them greets him and asks, "How's Marie?" Rodgers
responds that she is a bit wild. At this point he recog-
nizes that he has identified Marie with the boy, his
companion, who had gone off to the Fair. His friend
answers, "A *bit* wild! Come look at this!" He follows
the friend outside and, sorrowfully, sees several build-
ings burning. Marie has set them afire.

The dream extends an already clear pattern of Rodgers's confusions and feelings of impotence (not only
sexual) in relation to Marie—that much is certain, but
perhaps some speculation about specific elements would
be worthwhile. Rodgers's identification of the boy with
Marie indicates a double confusion: does he think of her
as a boy because he thinks of himself as a woman (as
he has in other dreams) or because of a homosexual
impulse? Probably both, but in either case his confusions about his sexual identity are manifest. He has
trouble getting over the wall because of his "burdens"
but the boy-Marie has no difficulty. This again sug-
gests, I think, Rodgers's sexual fear and confusion. He
envies the boy but as the boy is also Marie, he probably
also envies the boy-girl's lack of a "burden." Given

Rodgers's background, I think the May Fair represents the outside world or the pageant of life to him and is also of course associated with spring and sexuality. Therefore it is not surprising that the Marie-figure runs off to participate in it and enjoy it, while he is left behind. The examination of pipes seems obvious enough, as does the deliberation over whether to purchase one: does he have a penis or not? Further, the curious shapes of the bowls indicate more sexual confusion and make the pipes ambiguous male-female symbols. The last part of the dream continues to reflect Rodgers's feelings of powerlessness in relation to Marie and his fears of public disgrace. But it also no doubt expresses the wish that her "wildness" be known to everyone, perhaps so that he might escape blame for it.

Now without these dreams the outlines of Rodgers's situation are already clear, but with them one discerns a mind far more fragmented than outward circumstances or even Rodgers's poetry would suggest. The dream-atmosphere is one of pervasive terror, frustration, depression and despair—and I refer not only to the examples cited but to all his recorded dreams. What the dreams add most to our understanding of Rodgers is a connection between his general lack of a sense of identity and his lack of a sense of sexual identity. Who am I and what am I—Rodgers could answer neither question. And the longer he stayed with Marie, or so the dreams seem to indicate, the more those questions would torment him.

He used his writing as an instrument of sanity and as a means of extricating himself from Loughgall psychologically, preparatory to actual physical departure.

He must have been conscious of the entanglements of his sexual and professional doubts, because his poetry began to struggle toward a new paganism or romanticism, by which he hoped to overcome or at least get round his dilemmas. "When we are squeezed between two worlds and two flatly different loyalties," he reflected in 1954, "—one of flesh and one of faith—what else can the poet say but 'a plague on both your houses', and what else can he do but cock a snook at both? How else do we get ease and issue except by projecting a newborn world of the imagination which will comprehend and inherit the old ones but will override both—the world of poetry?"

The snook-cocking took two forms, a redefinition of pre-Christian, classical materials, and a redefinition of Christian materials. He tried to infuse both with his imagination and personality and thereby to create his own poetic world—and self-definition. He worked along these lines for many years, but the process began with three poems written between 1943 and '44—"Pan and Syrinx," "Apollo and Daphne," and "Lent." In the first, Rodgers makes use of the myth and of vigorous, sensual language and imagery to reformulate his favorite notions of perpetual clash and contrast. With Pan a goat and Syrinx a reed,

> Her he could feel, but never enter now;
> Him she could enter, but never feel:
> So red and green must wrangle endlessly.
> . . . Would nothing ease
> The nettle-tease of flesh, the salted taws
> Of lust?

In "Apollo and Daphne," he weaves his obsession with

the hunted hare into the myth, making Daphne the
hare and Apollo the hound, drawing from the classical
story another allegory of life's full circle.

But the most remarkable poem of the three, "Lent,"
takes Rodgers farthest towards that newborn world of
the poetic imagination. Writing about Mary Magdalene,
he turns the story of the Resurrection on its head:

> Mary Magdalene, that easy woman,
> Saw, from the shore, the seas
> Beat against the hard stone of Lent,
> Crying, 'Weep, seas, weep
> For yourselves that cannot dent me more.
>
> O more than all these, more crabbed than all stones,
> And cold, make me, who once
> Could leap like water, Lord. Take me
> As one who owes
> Nothing to what she was. Ah, naked.
>
> My waves of scent, my petticoats of foam
> Put from me and rebut;
> Disown. And that salt lust stave off
> That slavered me—O
> Let it whiten in grief against the stones
>
> And outer reefs of me. Utterly doff,
> Nor leave the lightest veil
> Of feeling to heave or soften.
> Nothing cares this heart
> What hardness crates it now or coffins.
>
> Over the balconies of these curved breasts
> I'll no more peep to see
> The light procession of my loves
> Surf-riding in to me
> Who now have eyes and alcove, Lord, for Thee.'
>
> 'Room, Mary,' said He, 'ah make room for me
> Who am come so cold now

To my tomb.' So, on Good Friday,
Under a frosty moon
They carried Him and laid Him in her womb.

A grave an icy mask her heart wore twice,
But on the third day it thawed,
And only a stone's-flow away
Mary saw her God.
Did you hear me? Mary saw her God!

Dance, Mary Magdalene, dance, dance and sing,
For unto you is born
This day a King. 'Lady,' said He,
'To you who relent
I bring back the petticoat and the bottle of scent.'

Strange thoughts from a parson. Christ reborn in Mary
Magdalene's womb, reborn when she relents and lets
thaw her lenten mask of self-denial; and for her warmth,
He returns to her the emblems of her sensuality and
bids her dance. The idea is quite close to that of D. H.
Lawrence in *The Man Who Died*, but in execution
Rodgers is more subtle and more lovely. He was getting
beyond himself, at last.

He did not deliver the poem from his pulpit, but it
was published (in the *New Statesman and Nation*) in
1945, after he had left Oxford and returned to Loughgall. What comment it caused in the parish I do not
know, but Rodgers had already stirred up a fuss with
another piece of heresy in the *New Statesman*, this one
political as well as religious. Shortly after settling down
in Oxford with Marie, he had visited the editor of the
New Statesman in London, to see about the possible
publication of some verse. Asked if he could write something about the religious situation in the North, he

said he could, and in November 1943, a little essay called "Black North" appeared. It was a witty, truthful and therefore inflammatory portrait of Catholic–Protestant divisions. Rodgers characterized the Catholics as democratic, progressive, emotional, sinuous, intuitive, and unstable; Protestants were more stable but also sarcastic, straight, puritanical, hypocritical, hieratic and committed to the established order. He professed equal affection for both sides and predicted that one day a new Irishman would be born out of the meeting of these two equals. But he castigated the ruling (and Protestant) Unionist Party for fomenting strife between the factions in order to keep power, using the border issue as a red-herring, and generally working against the best interests of all Irishmen.

If one keeps in mind that these charges against the Unionists are exactly the same as those made more recently by Miss Bernadette Devlin and the builders of the barricades in Derry and Belfast, one can get some idea of the reaction among the good Protestants of Loughgall in 1943. When Rodgers returned the next year, he noted that no bells rang to greet him and that though hands were out to him, eyes were averted from him. He asked his friend the horse-dealer what the matter was. "Damn the one," the horse-dealer said to his parson, "damn the one in these four townlands ever heard tell of the *New Statesman* afore. But no sooner was yon article of yours out than, dang it, if there weren't fifteen copies of the blasted thing flyin' like wasps round the parish. There's neither chick nor child that hasn't been stung into talk. It's a holy terror, I'm

telling you—the Lodges are fair flamin' and the men
are hardly to have or to hold. You should hear them,
the way they're gettin' on."

Rodgers calmed his flock so successfully that he was
elected, much to his embarrassment, to the local Unionist council, a post which he declined. But he must have
known the row the essay would create before he wrote
it. He did not write it merely to make trouble, but he
did want to begin putting some distance between himself and Loughgall simply by speaking his mind and
being himself, or, more accurately, finding himself.
His vision of a new Irishman and a new Ireland, neither
Protestant nor Catholic, came from the same source
as his desire to create a new poetic world, comprehend-
ing flesh and faith.

It is difficult to see how Rodgers, even had he been
able to endure the strife of his marriage and the psychological stress it aggravated, could have continued
as parson while publishing such essays as "Black North"
and such poems as "Lent." When Louis MacNeice
came over to Ireland late in 1944 to look for writers for
the new B.B.C. Third Programme, he sought Rodgers
out and offered him a job in London. Here was escape,
yet at first Rodgers balked. Loughgall was the landscape of his thoughts, wherever they were leading him;
it was the only landscape he knew. Then Marie started
to talk about going to Edinburgh to study psycho-
analysis and fate began to press his choice. He had
come to Loughgall to get away and to be left alone and
now he had to leave to be alone again. Lying under the
beech trees, "watching the daws launch themselves

from the topmost branches," he prayed for courage in
a poem:

THE FALL

> O angel of the ledges of our dread
> On whose jellied edges each joy is dangled
> Gently, like danger—now, like daws on trees
> Unbalancing, turn our dread into ease
> And let the fall open our wings' eyes wide
> In wonder at ourselves who were so slow
> To float out on the rootless raft of air
> With flowing hold.
> The Fall! the fall, from that safe tree
> Of love we so much feared to leave, elates
> And lifts our other selves to life. Only
> By daring do we learn our manyness.
> Safety stints us, turns us to stone, to one.
> This always-gibbering between fear and hope
> Doubles our life, and is the bloody pulse
> Of every vein. O angel of our dread,
> Delicately cater for us rough feeders
> Who ask a stone; and duly give us bread.

One can feel him trying to lift himself to flight, and
feel his fear that his wings might never open. He de-
liberated for over a year, trying to convince himself
of the many sides of his nature which waited to show
themselves forth, and finally, in 1946, he wrote to
MacNeice accepting the job and resigned his ministry.
It was to be a total break. He would go to London
alone, and not as a parson taking leave but simply as
a poet. Marie was to study in Edinburgh, the children
would stay behind with the aunts. "A seal," he felt,
"had been put on the past."

His last visitor was the neighboring Catholic priest,

offering his prayers and those of his people for whatever Rodgers might choose to do. And Rodgers preached his last sermon on the text, "By faith Abraham, when he was called to go out into a place which he should after receive as an inheritance, obeyed; and he went out, not knowing whither he went."

4
The Net

For about twenty years after the second world war, the
B.B.C. Third Programme provided for poets and poetry
as no broadcasting corporation has before or since.
Most British poets of any importance found employ-
ment there, some for long periods and others occasionally; they were assured of an audience a thousand times
larger than that for most books of poetry. The B.B.C.
was then as now an unwieldy and parsimonious bureau-
cracy, and salaries were minimal. But the Third Programme itself was staffed by people who in their work
cared first and last for the arts, and thus it was a far
more congenial place for poets than their present refuge,
the university.

Rodgers's immediate boss was Laurence Gilliam,
Head of Features, who encouraged his writers, producers and engineers to be as experimental and creative
as they could in the uses of broadcast sound. The idea
was to reach a new radio audience, a "third" audience,
to involve as performers and as listeners the most so-
phisticated elements of the population, and perhaps

to sophisticate the rest a bit along the way. There was an element of cultural evangelism in the Third Programme, so in a sense Rodgers moved from one ministry to another. But the atmosphere reminded him more of his first visit to Dublin than anything else. He loved the company of writers, actors, artists, musicians, the expanding rounds of friends and drinks, the long lunches and longer evenings in the George, the Stag, and the Dover Castle, favorite B.B.C. pubs near Broadcasting House. People and poetry had long been his passions, now he could indulge them entirely, listening and drinking and talking the days and nights.

No one who met Bertie Rodgers forgot the sound and sight of him. The general impression was of extreme physical fragility; you hoped he wouldn't fall down because he looked as though he might break. But the delicate air about him was due more to his voice, a wavering, slightly quavering tenor, and to his manner, courtly, tentative, graceful, somehow not of this world, than to his constitution, which was hardly enough to stand a night's drinking with the best the world has known—a Dylan Thomas or even a Brendan Behan. Rodgers's drinking was an extraordinary thing to behold. He was never ostentatious about it. He drank as he did everything else, quietly and sacramentally, glass upon glass in steady unmeasured procession, his talk dilating along with his arteries and filling the room like the smoke from his pipe. It was not the laconic talk one expects from a Protestant Ulsterman, not the kind of talk Rodgers used to illustrate by the story of the Catholic Ulsterman who said to the Protestant Ulsterman, "That's not a bad wee dog you have there."

"It never was meant to be a bad wee dog," replied the Protestant. Rodgers relished word-play, outrageous puns, stories that turned on a phrase. His supply of tales and wit was rich because, like most Irishmen, he forgot nothing; but he was adept too at the unrehearsed exchange. He used to enjoy trying to cheer up Dylan Thomas with talk, when Thomas was going through one of his desperate fallow periods. "I'm no bloody good," Thomas moaned one day at the George. "I'm only a stabbed grampus." "Ach, Dylan," Rodgers consoled him, "there are more stabs in the sea than grampuses that ever came out of it." And Thomas would be up and laughing for the moment at least. Or Rodgers would quote an old Ulster road-mender: "Ah well, God is good and the devil isn't bad, thank God."

It was his love of poets' talk and the gossip that makes up so much of it that led him to a splendid and original idea for a series of broadcasts. The memory of his first visit to Dublin was still fresh when he joined the gossipacious B.B.C. crowd, and he was reminded of the way the Dubliners had spun out their intricate and sinuous cobwebs of reminiscence, reticulations of facts and fantasies that had brought to life Irish writers of the past fifty years as books never could. To record some of this talk for a series of broadcasts on the Irish literary movement seemed an exciting prospect. Laurence Gilliam and the B.B.C. program planners agreed.

So it was that Rodgers became the oral historian of modern Irish literature. Oral history is a common enough pursuit these days, but when Rodgers began, the tape recorder had yet to be invented, and at first he and his producer, Maurice Brown, had to work with

those inefficient old wire machines. They had no broadcast precedents to help and inspire them, but Rodgers
knew just the sort of thing he wanted from the start.
He would make a series of broadcasts, each on a single
writer, each a collage of Irish talk. He began with Yeats
and moved on, between 1947 and '65, to Joyce, Synge,
Gogarty, AE, George Moore, F. R. Higgins, and Shaw.
There was also a program on Robert Flaherty, the
film director. For Rodgers the work could not have
been pleasanter. It meant seeking out the friends and
enemies and hangers-on of the great men, winning at
most their confidence but at least their candor, and
getting them to record the best and worst they could
remember. The result was a symposium of memories,
edited into rough chronological order, with gaps and
background filled in by Rodgers's narration. The
method, much copied once devised, became known
as the "Rodgers technique." Since nearly all the contributors were Irish, there was little trouble getting
them to talk, but little hope of getting them to tell the
truth. Rodgers took advantage of that problem, editing
so that contrary versions of the same story were jux-
taposed. The result was the fuller sort of truth that
only complementary lies can reveal. As he put it in his
preface to the forthcoming book version of the broadcasts, "I knew very well before I finished, how far any
man's statement was trustworthy or factual, but truth
is not the whole of life, or facts the whole of truth, and
these people were, like myself, as honest as the day is
long—and no more."

The broadcasts entailed many visits to Ireland and
Rodgers became familiar with the literary scene there,

past and present, as few men have, for he was part of
it as a poet yet usefully detached from it as its historian.
Everyone came to know him and, with his talent for
"crossing the counters," he made few enemies, though
several of the contributors became incensed at what he
permitted other contributors to say over the air. Joyce's
sister, Eva, for example, reproached him for allowing
Gogarty to describe her father as a drunkard. But when
Rodgers simply offered to let her refute Gogarty in
another broadcast, she could reply only, "James would
have liked you." Rodgers did, like everyone else in
Dublin, come under Patrick Kavanagh's lash. In a
broadside first published in the Dublin magazine *Envoy*
and now preserved in Kavanagh's *Collected Poems*,
Kavanagh asked "Who Killed James Joyce?", convicted
the author of a Harvard thesis, and inquired of the
assassin,

> How did you bury Joyce?
> In a broadcast symposium.
> That's how we buried Joyce
> To a tuneful encomium.
>
> Who carried the coffin out?
> Six Dublin codgers
> Led into Langham Place
> By W. R. Rodgers.
>
> Who said the burial prayers?—
> Please do not hurt me—
> Joyce was no Protestant,
> Surely not Bertie?

But, miraculously enough in Ireland, no one sued
Rodgers for libel, and the radio portraits were highly

esteemed. In 1951, in recognition of his poetry and of these broadcasts, he was elected to the Irish Academy of Letters, filling the vacancy left by the death of Shaw.

His other work for the B.B.C. was various—occasional verse; *The Return Room*, his play about his Belfast childhood; frequent "talks" or monologues which usually took the form of an Irish reminiscence but sometimes were little essays on the superstitions of fishermen, country patterns of life, the uses and abuses of doorknobs, and so forth. Most often, no matter what the topic, he would circle round to illustrate some aspect of Irish life and character, and for this there was always an anecdote—the old man, known for his pugnaciousness, lying on his deathbed gripping his favorite stick and saying to it, "Man dear, you and I have had a day and a half of it," then turning his face to the wall and breathing his last; or the fellow with the rabbit-waistcoat who noticed that every time his dog, who had killed the rabbit, approached, the hair on the waistcoat would stand straight up from fear. Listening to Rodgers's careful, artful speech, anyone could sense that he had collected stories like this all his life out of love for Irish life and Irish habits of mind, could sense the tethers that held him to Ireland no matter where he was. A familiar phenomenon with the Irish exile. One thinks of course of Joyce, with his map of Dublin, his picture of Cork framed in cork, his phoenix palms to remind him of the Phoenix Park.

One day in 1949, he was walking the streets of Armagh City, refreshing and gathering impressions for a radio portrait of the place, "City Set on a Hill." Just outside the Charlemont Arms Hotel, he en-

countered an elder of his former congregation. "Mr.
Rodgers," the elder said in surprise, "you'll have time,
maybe, for a wee sherry?" As minister he had never
been able to accept a drink in public, but now, he
thought with some pleasure, as an individual he could
do as he liked. He felt his own man. And so they went
into the lounge bar at the Charlemont. "Mr. Rodgers,"
said the elder firmly at the counter, "you'll have a big
whiskey." After two or three more big whiskeys, the
elder turned to him and said, "Mr. Rodgers, tell me
this and tell me it true, for the place is vacant now.
You wouldn't turn the collar and come back to us
again?" Rodgers thanked him. But "No," he said, "one
cannot go back on life."

It is a nicely paradoxical incident—his pleasure in
being himself, yet the curious, fatalistic wistfulness
about that last phrase. He had plenty of doubts and
guilts not to resolve about leaving Loughgall; they
often took the form of a daydream or nightdream about
the train which had carried him out of Armagh and
into his new life. That train went into a poem—

. . . The elbowing air
Ushers her on, cushions and repercussions her
In its indulgent hush. And always her weeping past
Wallabies wildly away in smokes and hang-
Overs of gloom across the long-ago fields that once were mine.
Long ago? No. The cataract still hangs
In tatters as it did. On the same thong of air
The hawk impends. Still leans the lonely tree
Above the only lake, its ageing shade
Unwrinkled in the shaking glass. And still
The fountain eyelashes a stony stare.
All's as I left it, place and pose and weather

That once was willed for ever. Once again
I look out from the train,·
I see the solemn child, and wave to it in vain.

The child was Harden, his elder daughter; her solemn
face was (and is) a feminine mirror-image of her
father's. For years he waved to her and to Nini vainly,
unable to bring himself to have them come live with
him in London, visiting them only rarely because of
the pain to himself. Of the pain to them he was only
too conscious and too paralyzed by his guilt. What the
B.B.C. listeners to his little talks about Ireland and
his days in Loughgall could not know was that each
time he visited the past he was touching present sorrows
and wondering what escape had cost.

Marie, meanwhile, having completed her psychoanalytic training in Edinburgh, held a succession of
positions in various hospitals in Scotland. But her own
health improved only sporadically, and she became
suicidal, making at least three attempts on her own
life. In 1953 she journeyed to Newcastle, County Down,
planning to visit her children, who were spending
their holidays nearby. But she collapsed among the
rocks near the sea, where she was found by a passing
motorist and taken to hospital. The strain, apparently,
had finally broken her, and she died within hours.
Rodgers came over for the funeral.

By that time he had been living for about a year with
Marianne Helweg, the former wife of Laurence Gilliam.
Rodgers had first met the Gilliams in April, 1945, when,
trying to decide whether to take the B.B.C. job, he
had visited them in London. When, a year later, he

arrived to begin his radio work, he stayed with them
in their house at Highgate for several months. He fell
in love with Marianne, and she with him. At this most
difficult point in his life, brought low with doubts
over past and future, he saw hope in her love, sympathetic and sensual. The differences between them—
she was Danish born, English educated, accustomed to
a life among artists—were important to him, since he
was trying to alter his life so drastically. She had been
on the staff of the B.B.C. Drama Department from
1933–'41, then at the European Service until 1943, after
which she left the B.B.C. but continued as a free-lance,
adapting and translating plays and writing documentary
programs on such figures as Van Gogh, Gauguin and
Strindberg. She was elegantly beautiful in a warm,
blonde Danish way. Their clandestine affair, lasting
seven years, became for Rodgers the attempt to achieve
in life what he had been trying to achieve in his poetry
—the transcendence of old fears and oppositions. His
poetry had started in this direction as early as 1943.
In 1950, he addressed this aggressively sensual—and
wonderfully successful—poem to Marianne:

THE NET

Quick, woman, in your net
Catch the silver I fling!
O I am deep in your debt,
Draw tight, skin-tight, the string,
And rake the silver in.
No fisher ever yet
Drew such a cunning ring.

Ah, shifty as the fin
Of any fish this flesh
That, shaken to the shin,

Now shoals into your mesh,
Bursting to be held in;
Purse-proud and pebble-hard,
Its pence like shingle showered.

Open the haul, and shake
The fill of shillings free,
Let all the satchels break
And leap about the knee
In shoals of ecstasy.
Guineas and gills will flake
At each gull-plunge of me.

Though all the Angels, and
Saint Michael at their head,
Nightly contrive to stand
On guard about your bed,
Yet none dare take a hand,
But each can only spread
His eagle-eye instead.

But I, being man, can kiss
And bed-spread-eagle too;
All flesh shall come to this,
Being less than angel is,
Yet higher far in bliss
As it entwines with you.

Come, make no sound, my sweet;
Turn down the candid lamp
And draw the equal quilt
Over our naked guilt.

I find the poem astonishingly good, not least of all in
the audacity and strangely, marvelously refreshing ob-
scenity of its metaphors. Marianne was astonished too.
She received it in a letter from Rodgers which she
opened innocently while breakfasting with friends, and
she had to run upstairs to digest it. The last stanza—
perhaps I mean the last word—keeps the poem honest,
for Rodgers. It is a shock to read "guilt" there, and it

reminds us of the moral and psychological limits on Rodgers's paganism. His second volume of poems, *Europa and the Bull*, published in 1952, bore the dedicatory couplet,

To M.

Come, Love; warm and widen me
From what I am to what I'll be.

There was much gossip about who M might be, since Rodgers was no longer living with his wife. But he provided an obscure hint that, whoever she was, she could not be Marie by placing a passage from the *Purgatorio*, Canto I, alone and in the original, just before the text of his own poems begins. The passage is a portion of Cato's speech to Dante and Virgil, in which Cato gives the pair permission to proceed and tells Virgil to bathe Dante's face of all defilements, so that he may be a fit traveller toward paradise. All this would be mystifying, were it not that in the preceding passage, which Rodgers cautiously left out, Cato tells of his repudiation of his wife, Marcia, for the sake of the heavenly woman, the embodiment of divine truth, Beatrice. Rodgers is telling any reader who can figure it out that Marie is his Marcia, the new M his Beatrice, and that he, like Cato and Dante, struggles by the light of a woman through purgatory toward, if not paradise, then peace.

Not even Marianne was aware of the significance of the passage from Dante. But when Rodgers went off to live with her, everyone could at last be sure who M. was. And Laurence Gilliam said, "She may make him happy, but he will not write any more poetry."

5

The Swan

Europa and the Bull comprises all of the poems Rodgers
wrote between 1941 and 1952, 28 of them, including
the 500-line title poem and the 250-line "Resurrection:
An Easter Sequence." He had arrived in England in
1946 with about 18 finished poems in his luggage. One
can draw what conclusions one likes from this fact.
Some of Rodgers's Irish friends and relatives point to
it to argue that he ought never to have left Loughgall,
but surely they overlook not only the psychological
pressures impelling his departure but that with such
unparsonish poems as "Lent" he was preparing his way
out by the act of writing. The shocks of his new life
obviously took time to absorb. He felt himself, as he
wrote in "The Trinity," a house divided between "The
nagging cat of thought, the mouse/Of niggling guilt . . ."
Yet he knew that without such tensions, he would have
little impetus to write at all.

Most of the poems had already appeared in periodi-
cals and newspapers—in *Horizon, The New Statesman,*

The Listener, Botteghe Oscure, Poetry Quarterly, The Bell, The Irish Times, and *Lagan.* Three had been written for and broadcast over the B.B.C. In a rather hostile review in the *Listener,* Roy Fuller mocked the inclusion of these radio pieces as somehow beneath the dignity of *ars poetica* and as a sign of the incoherence of the collection. He speculated that Rodgers must have had difficulty putting it all together. Fuller was right about the difficulty but mistaken about the reasons for it and wrong about the quality of the poems written for radio. Rodgers's self-confidence had not been such as to facilitate the completion of a new volume. Even when he had almost all of it done, in 1950, he could not bring himself to complete the final tidying up nor to get the poems into logical rather than chronological order. Mrs. Wyn Henderson, who had given advice and help and the comfort of intelligent understanding to many poets, among them Dylan Thomas, took Rodgers into her house in Mecklenburg Square, Bloomsbury, for two years and got him to finish the job. Years before she had run her own press, had founded the Aquila Press and had been Production Manager for the Nonsuch Press and for Nancy Cunard's The Hours Press in the early 1930s. A woman without prejudice and with a remarkable sympathy for the artistic temperament, she put Rodgers's papers in order for him and saved his book from its slough of doubt and drink. Fuller's reaction to it was singular. The other reviews were all enthusiastic, and while G. S. Fraser, in the *New Statesman,* did see incoherence in Rodgers's occasionally colloquial treatment of religious subjects, no one but Fuller singled out the B.B.C. poems as inferior.

What could have been taken for incoherence or incongruity was in fact the keystone of Rodgers's art. His primary obsession in writing was the word itself, and the sound of the word as much or more than its sense. He used to say, playfully yet seriously, that he cared more about *sound* sense than sound *sense*. If the *sound* sense conveyed two or three meanings, even contradictory ones, so much the better, because so much the more true to life. The anonymous reviewer for the *Times Literary Supplement* understood this aspect of Rodgers very well and placed him in sympathetic company with Dylan Thomas, W. S. Graham, and others he termed, in the heading of his front-page article, "The New Romantics." (How gratifying, to leave the service of Calvin's God and have one's new allegiance proclaimed approvingly on the front page of the most important of literary journals.) The new romantic was characterized as taking an intuitive approach to art as to life, as unwilling to submit to external disciplines, scorning consecutive reasoning, probing life instead in all its rich, Keatsian profusion. He "transfers his emotions to the page by the alchemy of spitting or singing words" which produces a "heady emotional effect." He tries to impart "no 'message' nor assayable panacea; nothing can be cut from his poems, and dried, and quoted in adage form for the castigation of the conscience." His poetry is for those who "accept life in all its manifestations." Rodgers was an important link between the old and the new, combining a liking for classical subjects, an intense preoccupation with wry wit and word-play, with an ebullient and intuitive welcoming of life. When dealing with religious subjects, he was confident, dramatic, and appealingly "familiar." "Here is richness, here is sensual enjoyment. . . . There is a lazy mastery about Mr. Rodgers at his best."

All of which must have been especially pleasing to Rodgers because true. The preachiness of *Awake!* was gone, the verbosity brought under greater control, the invention and luxuriance of language retained and refined. One gets a sense if not of a resolution of conflicts then of a delicate, fluid equilibrium among them; a sense of the poems, like Rodgers's swan, holding "the heavens, shores, waters and all their brood."

The most ambitious poem, "Europa and the Bull," is too long, but it has magnificent moments and often becomes a truly exalted piece of writing. Epic in style and scope, spanning seas and continents, its main action an enormous act of sexual intercourse, it revolves around the ancient question of man's relationship to God, of how much God there is in man and how much animal, the question asked by all myths in which God takes the form of man or animal.

> . . . Seeing him assume
> That luminous image, did she divine
> The blind milennium of mind behind
> The upstart moment, the deep duplicity
> Of flesh and spirit, clod and cloud, the make-and-break
> Of clamouring animal and calm god,
> And man the amalgam?
>
>   .   .   .
>
> Look how in this one man
> The animal ran on, the god drew back

From brute rapacity, reining and rearing,
Yet the tormenting rub and rob between
Was itch and ecstasy to him.

G. S. Fraser, in his review, wrote of Rodgers's "sacramentalisation of sex"; he may have been thinking of this poem, as well as of "The Net" and others. For in his narration of the abduction of Europa, daughter of Cadmus, by Zeus, who takes the form of a bull, Rodgers endows their coupling with the significance of the celebration of the mass, when Word becomes flesh, God becomes man. Here God becomes animal and enters woman, mingling with her, comingling with her flesh and spirit, and through this act—tender and violent, brutal and delicate—heaven and earth are joined. The poem implies that the act of love in sex and sex in love can unite the sundered halves of our natures as can nothing else, implies this, does not preach this, making it happen in words—

O how the blush belled in her body now,
And how the confused water of her wits
Began to cloud and boil.
He from her confusion took delight,
She from his joy took more confusion still,
And still the dizzy circle swirled them in
And swung them up in swings of argument
And roundabout agreement. Each way they swayed
And swirled alternately, were two and one
By turns, opposed and yet appeased:
And, in between, the pulsing spirit flowed
In threads of love . . .

The poem sighs to a close in one of the softest, loveliest passages I know of in modern poetry, sinking over the sleeping pair quietly as nightfall:

May sleep after sleep, loved over by leaves,
Engross those two, house them and hush them
In arms of amaranth,
And may the nodding moth of myth
In every mouth take breath and wing now,
And dance these words out in honour of that wedding.

The theme of "Europa and the Bull" runs through many poems in the volume, if we can take that theme broadly as the divine in the human and the human in the divine. "The Journey of the Magi" offended some reviewers because of its extremely colloquial language. It is a question of personal taste, whether one likes to see the three kings portrayed as well-intentioned bumblers, not really sure where the hell they are going; but if one can see the human in the divine, the poem is ingratiating and amusing. And more—because Rodgers has the kings find not just a heavenly child, but what they had no idea they were looking for—

It was the child within themselves
For which they'd sought, for which Age delves
—Now Age and Innocence can meet,
Now, now the circle is complete,
The journey's done. Lord, Lord, how sweet!

It is much the same in all the Christian poems, of which there are six, including the fourteen parts of the "Resurrection" sequence. Rodgers portrays "Christ walking on the Water" as an entirely human figure, losing all confidence of purpose, ending up "Curled like a question mark asleep." And in the various sections of "Resurrection," each based on a passage from the King James version, the emphasis is always on the simple, immediate, and human, as is the language. As an example take Rodgers's commentary on Judas:

> Name him not, Name him not, nor constellate
> The one who led him to his fate. Nevertheless
> Judas was part of Jesus.
> For the god always has a foot of clay, and the soul
> Grows in soil, the flower has a dark root.
> And deep in all is the base collaborator.
> The betrayer is always oneself, never another.
> All must say, 'Lord is it I?' There is always
> Evil in Goodness, lust in love, dust on the dove's foot,
> And without it purity's groundless. And the Cross
> Had never been.

Or take the simplicity of Rodgers's description of Christ on the cross:

But when you come up against it all good words about it
Are less than breath. It is hard to turn the other cheek
When both have been slapped:

> Yes, it was a hard death.

These verses were written for a special B.B.C. international hookup program broadcast Easter Sunday 1949. Rodgers had been asked to provide some sort of "links" between the various segments of the program, which was to switch from one European capital to another—the Sokol Choir singing in Prague one moment, other voices from Paris the next, and so forth. He took the assignment quite seriously and came up with a sequence of poems so affecting that, in the words of someone who heard the broadcast, with Rodgers reading his own lines, "it was like another crucifixion." Rodgers often grumbled about the pressures of his B.B.C. work,

but in this instance, they spurred him to something
fine, which he would otherwise not have done, and gave
us proof that writing need not be base when written for
a mass audience.

As I scan the table of contents of *Europa and the
Bull*, I am struck by the quality of Rodgers's achievement and by the extent to which the poems represent
personal triumphs for him. As in any collection, there
are peaks and valleys, but not a single poem I should
as soon see thrown out. Even the less interesting ones
earn their keep with lines and metaphors worth cherish-
ing. "Autumn Day," for instance, does little more than
convey a scene, but I want to remember

The rooks dying and settling like tea-leaves over the trees;
And, rumbling on rims of rhyme, mine were the haycarts
    home-creeping
Leaving the rough hedge-checks long-strawed and streaked
    with their weeping.

"Summer Journey" provides a good example of how
intriguing and pleasurable Rodgers's poems—even the
minor ones—can be. In the summer of 1947 Rodgers
took a continental holiday with Maurice Brown, one
of his B.B.C. producers. The trip covered several coun-
tries, but in the poem, which was commissioned by
the B.B.C., Rodgers confines himself to a single Sunday
in the Pays-Basque. As simple description the poem
is wonderful and it gives one an idea of what Rodgers
might have done had he turned more often to subjects
unfamiliar to him. The heat, the color and the smell
of that Basque Sabbath are conveyed with great intensity. But the thematic complications of "Summer

Journey" are, for me at least, most impressive of all.
The poem praises the Basques in the spirit of *carpe
diem*:

> Happy people. No greed for tomorrow
> Greys your face like frost. O
> May all your valleys be fat
> With wine, and full be every vat.

And as each activity of the day is traced—from early
mass, to dancing and game-playing, to the final drinking
and singing in cafés—one gathers a strong sense of the
immediacy of these people and of how they do live for
the present, for the moment. The "bridegroom-priest"
before a "blaze of incense and a bloom/ Of candles";
the yellow houses, shaded by chestnut and lime trees;
the dancers, red-sashed, cool and clean; the *"pock"* of
the *pelota* ball; the "two old dignified men . . . battling
over a bottle/ Twisting in wordy wedlock like eels . . .";
all these things, these images seize this day for us, as
the people who lived it seized it.

But into this present scene, Rodgers weaves con-
figurations of eternity, so that the very immediacy of
the day becomes a symbol and a microcosm of time's
passing.

> And the village fête on Sunday where we saw
> The circle of life complete, saw the day
> Turn from morning to night, from light to grey,
> And the people counterwise from grave to gay,
> From church to dance and then from dance to play.

The day, then, is one time and all time. And further,
within each specific activity Rodgers identifies a sign
of something larger than the thing itself. The mass, of

course, is "the Mystery/ That has been all men's history." The women singing below and the men, "galleried," responding from above are heaven and earth in dialogue. When the curé comes out to watch the dancers, or a priest plays the pipe or sweeps "in magpie flight" black-robed among the white-clad *pelota*-players, it is a sign of the Church's entering the world:

> Yes. This morning the world went into the church.
> Now the church comes into the world. So,
> In life we oppose and appease each other.

The dance tells of the rise and fall of summer,

> Needle-pipe and thimble-drum
> Leading the way to kingdom come.

Finally the moon comes up and looks down upon

> Outlay and intake of breath, rise and fall
> Of a season, ins and outs of a dance.

And the poem, like the day, is done, containing within itself—everything, it seems: yesterday and tomorrow in that single Sabbath day.

There are more perfect poems than "Summer Journey," but few richer. And at his best, Rodgers is quite simply first-rate by any measure. "The Net" stands comparison with the boldest and wittiest of metaphysical and cavalier roguery, while such poems as "Lent" and "Neither Here nor There" (like "Beagles" and "Paired Lives" from *Awake!*) are originals, tours-de-force, which lend themselves not to comparison but surely and simply to any list of poems in English deserving of immortality. "Europa and the Bull" is more difficult to evaluate. It does feel padded in spots, and one would like to delete a few over-clever phrases, but it achieves a sustained, an epic lyricism which blurs its flaws. A very good poet who wrote a few great poems, a poet whose talent was obviously so fine that one dearly wishes he had written more.

He did write more, but only a bit, and one can guess why. His consciousness of the circle of life was greater than his concern for fame or even for private achievement in poetry. There is a poem in *Europa* called

THE TOWER

Pile upon pile of thought he drove
Into the sobbing bog below,
While others on the shaking raft
Of laughter traveled to and fro;
Light after light of love sailed by
His single and unseeing eye.

Coldly he willed and boldly strove
To build the lean and winding stair,
While, wide and high, the idle drove
Swung on hyperboles of air;
In hopes of happiness they curled
Bat-like about his darkening world.

Whose was the hand that laid the pyre?
What was the foot that fled the stair?
Look how the jarring tongues of fire
Roll out and glory-hole the air.
From the charred arches of his brain
The golden girders fall like rain
Upon the unforgiving plain.

We think of Yeats, of his Tower, and of his lines, "The intellect of man is forced to choose/ Perfection of the life or of the work . . ." Rodgers's poem gives us his own image of the man who chooses the work, building his tower while laughter and love pass by, only to have his brain-palace burn down around him at the end. So many of his other poems celebrate a day, a season, an evanescent moment; and so much of his life was an effort to seize the raft of laughter and the lights of love. It could even be said that he wrote his poems in the service of his own salvation and not at all to raise some literary and intellectual edifice. What his poems cost him was the price of self-liberation. Once free, and we are the poorer for it, he ceased payment.

6

Neither Here Nor There

"All round me in Essex is a wide, quiet, flat corn-growing countryside with fields so big that, if you were to go into one end of a field as a young man, you would come out at the other end as an old man. And the people too are flat and endless as the fields. By which I mean to say that there are no great ups-and-downs in them, no sudden dramatic changes, no peaks of passion or drops of despair. They are level people who are used to looking into long distances of time. . . . And that, of course, is why I choose to live here. If occasionally I visit my native country, Ireland, to find clash and colour, I come back to Essex to find peace."

He wrote that in 1963, after almost eleven years' living in Sussex and Essex—at Stoke-by-Nayland, Borley, Ardleigh, and Colchester. The passage comes from a little book privately printed in Colchester, *Essex Roundabout*, which reads very much like his B.B.C. talks sounded, full of anecdotes, overheard conversations, two or three poems—a charming book, with a peaceful tone to it that hints that he had found at least some of the peace he sought.

Rodgers and Marianne chose to live in the country partly to escape the press of the B.B.C. crowd, not all of whom had been pleased by their love affair and, in 1953, their marriage. But they both enjoyed the country life, and it was good to be able to have houses big enough for various visitors, among them Rodgers's sister Reah, who came with her three children to live with them at Ardleigh in 1960, after the death of her first husband. The three children from Marianne's first marriage, Nina, John, and William, were there, and in 1956 a daughter, Lucy, was born to them. Rodgers's two other daughters remained, except for visits, in Ireland—at Banbridge Academy, County Down, still in the care of the aunts. Harden went on to Trinity College, Dublin, and a doctorate in English literature from Cambridge; Nini to Queen's University, Belfast, and her doctorate in history there.

Rodgers continued writing, but few poems: I am aware of six between 1952 and his death; there may be others, but not many. Instead he confined himself to his B.B.C. work and to reviews and essays for *The Listener, The New Statesman, The Sunday Times, The Observer*, and *The Irish Times*. I believe I have read most of the reviews—forty or so in all. In not one of them have I discovered a harsh criticism. The faintly negative comment is rare enough and is always isolated in an otherwise favorable notice. The reason for this does not lie in either an absence of critical faculty or an unearthly sweetness of temper. In private, as I later discovered for myself, Rodgers could be acid, often hilariously so, in his remarks about other people's books. His private opinion of Richard Ellmann's biography of Joyce, for example, was a low one, yet he praised the book unequivocally in *The Listener*. The truth is that he feared getting harsh treatment himself and felt that he should do unto other books as he wished done to his. He had a passion not to do public hurt to another. I once heard him scold Conor Cruise O'Brien for having blasted a book about the Irish Rebellion by a young American scholar. "I care about that subject," said O'Brien, "and I don't see why the man's ignorance should be excused just because of youth. He is misinforming people."

"That's no cause," Rodgers replied, "to give the poor fellow pain. He's a nice man." After which he placed a copy of a book I had written on Joyce into O'Brien's hands and urged him to help me by giving it a good review. Fortunately, O'Brien had been sufficiently affected by Rodgers's remonstrance not to review my book at all.

For the B.B.C. he continued to work on his portraits of Irish writers, including one program of the reminiscences of Richard Best, the librarian of the National Library, who appears in *Ulysses*. In addition, there were programs on "The Bare Stones of Aran," the Abbey Theatre, and, to commemorate the fiftieth anniversary of the 1916 Easter Rebellion, a program called "Old Ireland Free." After 1957, he contributed regularly to a morning magazine program, "Today."

He also wrote, in addition to *Essex Roundabout*, the text for *Ireland in Colour*, first published in 1957 and reprinted in 1963. Perhaps his words were supposed to supplement the photographs, but the little essays which he composed about various sections of the country are, to my mind, the best prose written in this century about the physical characteristics of Ireland. He had another such project in progress for many years with Louis MacNeice and a contract from Oxford University Press for it. Called *The Character of Ireland*, the book was to tell of various aspects of national life, from religion to sports and pubs. The two of them began work on it in 1952 and finished the text in two or three years. MacNeice was to write a poem for the beginning and Rodgers one for the end. MacNeice finished his. Rodgers kept promising his. From time to time the text had to be revised, because information about such things as sports kept getting out of date. The publisher never gave up hope of receiving Rodgers's poem, and he kept the book on ice for a decade or so. Rodgers never wrote the poem.

After years of living alone and years of domestic warfare before that, his literary ambitions were not such as to rouse him from the peace of his new life. Amid the frequent chaos among different children of different families in his house, he appeared oblivious, withdrawn, serene. He was sufficiently haunted by the past, moreover, not to want to probe into it and into himself with poetry's blade. From time to time at night —and this went on until his death—he would, after a quantity of drink, work himself into a terrible rage against women and what he imagined they had done and were doing to him. In his fury he would rave at Marianne while calling her Marie: the past had him about the throat. But his love and need for Marianne were strong. He did not like her to be away for long, and though they could have used the money, he refused

to let her take a job which would require her absence
during the day. Once, Marianne went into London to
do some research at the British Museum Reading Room.
He grumbled about her going. She had been there a
few hours when an attendant came over and said there
was a gentleman to see her outside. There on a bench
sat Rodgers, sheepish perhaps but quite sure he was
in his rights to see what Marianne was "up to" and to
bring her back at once. She refused to go.

In 1965, they began to think of going to America
for a year or two, inspired by the example of many
other writers who were taking advantage of the good-
will and good money offered by American universities
and colleges. He made a few inquiries to no avail when
Mrs. Esther Wagner, of Pitzer College in Claremont,
California, offered him a visiting professorship at a
salary munificent by British standards. Mrs. Wagner,
who knew and admired Rodgers's work, had written
to him immediately upon learning of his availability
through Herbert Howarth, of the University of Pennsyl-
vania. The Rodgerses had never heard of either Mrs.
Wagner or of Pitzer, a small women's college, part of
an associated group of six called the Claremont Colleges;
but the job seemed agreeable enough, Mrs. Wagner
would take care of everything, including housing, and
California had obvious attractions. They arrived in
Claremont in the fall of 1966.

At the time I was in my second year of teaching at
Pomona College, another in the Claremont group. I
remember well my first meeting with him. Dick Barnes,
a colleague of mine, and his wife, Kate, had invited
me to lunch at their house with the Rodgerses. When

I arrived, Rodgers arose to greet me, a glass of Guinness in his hand, and commented immediately on my name. "That is the real thing," he said, slowly, ominously, looking me over as though to see what Irish traces were left after three generations of debasement. I tried to explain that it was really quite inauthentic, that my mother, a snob, despised the Irish and had tried to balance the O'Brien with what she thought was both Jane Austen and French. "But you know that Darcy is a very old Irish name," he said. I did. "Well then," he said to me, "it shows your mother couldn't stop what had to be"—this with a conspiratorial smile, as if to confirm that a great and mysterious bond had been revealed, linking me to 800 years of underground struggle against the conqueror.

He was quiet during lunch; afterwards came bourbon and a loosening of tongues. Rodgers was one of the greatest talkers who ever lived. But he required something of his listeners. He never filled in the backgrounds, never bothered with transitions, and if you lost the drift of his speech, there was no catching up with it. I think it was a kind of test of his: "Do you get me?" his eyes would ask. "If you do, come along. If you don't, to hell with your ignorance anyway." At this first meeting, I was uninitiated and prone stupidly to ask for clarifications. I also confess that I began by commenting on the warmth of California in September. To which came the reply,

RODGERS: Gogarty was the most generous man I ever knew.

MYSELF: Gogarty. *The* Gogarty?

RODGERS: A most generous man. Not at all the way that book made him out.

MYSELF: (Triumphantly.) You mean *Ulysses*.

RODGERS: I first met him in a busy English pub. I was so caught by his fine and scandalous talk that I watched a stranger beside me steal my overcoat, without so much as registering the fact.

MYSELF: That's awful. Did you get it back?

RODGERS: Still, if talk had been cloth I'd have had the makings of an overcoat.

MYSELF: If?

RODGERS: No more gifted raconteur came out of that city than Gogarty at his best. He could put the word on it. He had the poet's ear for words. He told me the time Yeats, as an old man, had come back from Spain where he was wintering for the good of his health. He brought with him a letter from his Spanish doctor, addressed to Gogarty, his Dublin doctor. Gogarty opened the letter and read it. It said: "We have here an antique cardio-sclerotic of advanced age." "Well," says Gogarty to me, "I knew it was a death sentence—heart disease—so I shoved the letter quickly into my pocket. 'No no,' said Yeats, 'you must read me that letter, Gogarty. After all, it's my funeral.' "

So, very reluctantly, Gogarty got out the letter and read the final words: "We have here an antique cardio-sclerotic of advanced age." Yeats rolled the words over and over on his tongue—"Cardio-sclerotic . . . cardio-sclerotic . . . Cardio-sclerotic . . . Do you know, Gogarty," said he, "I would rather be called 'cardio-sclerotic' than 'Lord of Lower Egypt!' "

MYSELF: (The sort of laugh you give when you think something is funny but you know it is even funnier than you think it is.)

RODGERS: Gogarty had that ear for words too. You could hear it in the way he told the story. The pure delight in the sound of words which can enable a man to pick the eye out of death itself.

MYSELF: (Drinks.)

RODGERS: Do you know that when he found my overcoat was stolen he peeled off his and pushed it into my hands? "No doubt," he said, "your wallet has gone too." And he pulled off a straggle of pound notes and forced them on me.

MYSELF: Amazing. *Was* your wallet gone?

RODGERS: I mentioned this later to Mrs. Yeats.

MYSELF: ?

RODGERS: She wasn't surprised. She didn't care if he talked scandal. Not a bit. The kindest heart in Dublin and the dirtiest tongue.

MYSELF: Scandal.

RODGERS: "Don't you know," she said, "that a man may do that and still be the most loyal friend you ever had?"

And Rodgers fixed a look on me that made me think that he knew that I talked scandal, or told me that he talked scandal, or said that we could be friends all the same.

I heard Rodgers practice variations on these and countless other anecdotes many times during the next two and a half years, and no doubt his B.B.C. audience heard them before I did. Each time he repeated them, I delighted in them more, because each time I could follow them better and relish the confusion of a new listener.

He was often at the Barneses. Kate is herself a poet, Dick a poet and a scholar; Bertie felt at ease with them in their sprawling hilltop house, with the dogs and horses and chickens that stroll in and out of it. At night he and Marianne would sit with the Barneses drinking and talking, and sometimes Kate would sing ballads for them, but more often Dick would take him out to one and another of the Mexican bars you can find, if you are with Barnes, in that part of Southern California —small, battered places, with beer on the floor and maybe a pool table. Bertie loved these excursions. He would astound and endear the locals—mostly working men—with his frail, precise, mysterious manner, his stories, and his capacity for beer. The pubs, as Bertie called them, stay open very late in California.

It is ironic that, after joining the ministry to avoid regular hours and leaving the ministry to be freer still, Rodgers was faced at the end of his rope with meeting classes. When I dropped in on his classes from time to time, he would glance up at me forlornly from behind his lectern and nod ceremoniously, always with that hint of conspiracy, looking for all the world like the interned refugee once again. But he had worked out an enviable system of teaching. The first thirty minutes would be taken up by one of his B.B.C. tapes. Then, the class sufficiently awed by hearing the voices of people they had scarcely conceived of as real, happy in the presence of a man who had actually spoken to these ghosts, he would string out an instructive anecdote till the bell. He spoke to his students as he always spoke, a slight, oracular tremor in his voice. He would begin, "An old woman in the West told me once . . ." or "There was the time that Paddy Kavanagh . . ." and he would end, "And that was the way it was then in the days when . . ." In fact he enjoyed these classes and felt as though he had regained his flock without having to preach of sin and salvation. As for the students, they loved him, always filling the large lecture hall, some of them coming to me to find out more about this strange Irishman. But when I told them he was a wonderful poet, they wondered why they had not heard of him.

Some of his colleagues weren't believers either. Mrs. Wagner, who had protected him the first year, left to teach at California Polytechnic College after that, and Rodgers was left prey to academic regimentation and its enforcers. Papers, examinations, grades: if they were condemned to all this, Rodgers had damn well be condemned to it too. This in a College only a couple of years old, which prided itself on its freedom from accepted systems, which boasted of its experimental programs, its democratic "decision-making-process," and so forth. However free a place it was, it was not free enough to let Rodgers alone.

He, of course, was adept at passive resistance. He would simply let the papers pile up on his desk and bulge his briefcase, week after week, treating them like messages from another world he could not possibly communicate with, until, the semester at an end and the registrar threatening excommunication, he could say, "You see, I have all these papers. Will it be all right about the papers?" And if his overlords wanted

them done, they had to help him. But the pressure
bothered him and wore him down. He had no wish to
make things difficult for others, yet he was not going
to submit to their efforts to make things difficult for
him. It was a battle. And as Monsignor Paddy Browne,
lying on his deathbed, had said to him years before,
"You, Rodgers, are a battlement!"

He was happiest in Claremont during the week of
his Irish Festival, which ended on St. Patrick's Day 1968.
In a way the Festival was his revenge on the academic
blockheads who had too often treated him like just
another professorial slave. He had had another good
idea too: this was the notion of starting an Irish collection in the library. Funds were insufficient, he argued,
to build up a decently comprehensive library, so why
not specialize? He could tell them what to buy. What
a marvellous collection it could have been, and with it
Rodgers could have left a permanent legacy to California. But the College officials could not possibly
admit that their library was not already catching up on
the Bodleian, nor did they know enough either about
Rodgers or Irish literature to see what he had in mind,
so his idea was rejected. "I am very angry," he said
after that. "I am very angry indeed."

With the Irish Festival he took no chances. Some-
how, and I have no idea how, he and his ally, Professor
Carl Hertel, got a grant for their scheme from the State
Department. Money in hand, Rodgers invited the
Conor Cruise O'Briens, Benedict Kiely and Herbert
Howarth, author of *The Irish Writers*. "They will all
come here," said Rodgers, "to see me dead, but won't
they be shocked to see me alive." There were films and

plays; readings by Máire MacEntee, Barnes, and Rodgers; and lectures by Kiely, Howarth, and O'Brien. Through it all, Rodgers presided with an air of consummate satisfaction, as if to say, "You see? You see?" He was never so ebullient. Normally a paltry and picky eater (after once tasting a California vegetable, he never did so again because he said they tasted of nothing), he arranged pre-performance feasts at pretentious restaurants and gourmandized like Edward VII himself, urging us on to more food and more bottles, reminding us that the American Government was paying, toasting Dean Rusk again and again: "A much maligned man. Look what he has given us. Ben, give me your glass." There was a dinner at his own house as well, after which he and Kiely sang ballads in the Tyrone dialect—

> Me da lived up in Carmin
> And he kep' a servant-boy,
> The second wife was very short,
> He buried her wi' joy.

And there was a loud, long party in an abandoned saloon, with a near fist-fight at the end. O, a lovely time! The liquor bill for the five days was a thousand dollars.

His attitude to Conor Cruise O'Brien is revelatory of how one kind of Irishman deals with another kind of Irishman. He cherished O'Brien as an old friend, was sympathetic to his politics, admired his writing. Yet he was rather fearful and distrustful of O'Brien's intellect. "Conor," he said to me, "has the best mind to come out of Ireland in our time. He can take an argu-

ment and cut it up seven thousand ways." His words
were full of awe, but it was almost as though he had been
warning me to beware the foul fiend. O'Brien was too
rational. Around him Rodgers had the air of a man
half-expecting to be ambushed. It was all fantasy, of
course. After he had seen the O'Briens off at the airport,
he said to my wife and me, "Never have two friends
been so glad to see one another, and so glad to say
good-bye to one another," and urged the necessity of
repairing immediately to the bar. The day before, however, when O'Brien had delivered his lecture, exercis-
ing his brilliant persuasiveness and wit upon the audience, Rodgers had looked the proud father, though
O'Brien was but seven years his junior.

With Benedict Kiely, Rodgers felt more relaxed. The
two of them sat in my apartment till four in the morning, engaged in an undeclared drinking, singing and
talking contest. They went on and on long after the
rest of us were stocious. Rodgers won. Kiely gave up
when, wagging a finger at him, Rodgers warned, "Do
you know that I was a Presbyterian minister in County
Armagh for twelve long years!" I accompanied Kiely
back to his motel. He kept muttering, "I'm a beaten
man, beaten, beaten. Bertie Rodgers you out-talked me
you out-drank me Bertie Rodgers . . ."

In the most appealing way, Rodgers regarded himself as an Irish missionary to America—his church neither Presbyterian nor Roman but Irish, its liturgy all
of Irish culture, its saints the Yeatses and the Joyces.
That is the chief reason, aside from the fun of it, that
he threw himself into his Festival with such devotion.
Most of the time in Claremont, though he enjoyed the

informal, easy way of life, he suffered the loneliness of
the exile. Perhaps a few appreciated the importance of
his past accomplishments, his books and his broadcasts;
only a handful knew enough about Ireland—or cared
enough—to appreciate the spirit of what he was saying
or his own spirit. Looking at him, one often got a
painful sense of a man knowing, and knowing that no
one else knew.

For his part, he absorbed and once turned into words
the physical and cultural landscape around him. Here
is a portion of a poem of his inspired by the candidacy
of Dr. Max Rafferty, the prominent California educator,
for the United States Senate:

LAMENT FOR AN EDUCATED HOLE IN THE ROAD

Some creep stole a hole last night
Out of our L.A. freeway . . .
A hole is a full-stop, a think-tank
A night-stick for eggheads, highbrows, cleaver-pushers,
Sour-grapepickers, protestors, and all damn fools
Who want bread on their jam. Actually
There's no knowing what a hole's about;
That is the beauty of it.
A hole is silence, is topless. . . .
                    Look at it
In the round, just. A hole is an O, like in
Order, cop, property-lot, politics,
Oil, development, motivation, goal.
It is the mouthpiece of democracy. . . .

He wrote the poem in the fall of 1968. I first saw the
manuscript when my wife and I were sitting with
Marianne and him in his study, a bright, spare room,
nicely scattered over with books, odds and ends of
manuscripts, copies of the *T.L.S.*, *The Listener*, the

Irish Times. He made a practice of clipping out articles which interested him—reviews, a new theory of time which seemed to correspond to the timeless stasis he wrote about in "Neither Here nor There"—and these were about in little piles. Marianne was having a gin; for us and himself he opened a quart of bourbon and, with ceremony, he slowly filled our glasses, and then his own, to the brim. The bottle was empty in an hour and a half. At this point, he went to his desk and pulled out the manuscript of "Lament for an Educated Hole." We read it, laughing, and asked where it was going to be published. He said he hadn't thought about it. What about the student newspaper? I said this was rather a lowly place for it, but he disagreed. The students would enjoy it and he liked the idea of giving Dr. Rafferty a punch in the nose in the local press. I said I'd see that it got to the paper and staggered to my car. Later I discovered he had given another copy to Barnes to deliver to another local paper. My copy got published first; the other paper was furious. Rodgers relished the row and denied any responsibility for it.

Whatever his sense of exile, he wanted to stay in California for the full three years of his visa. The climate was agreeable, he had a decent salary for the first time in his life. He and his wife had made friends and had found a fine house—a big rustic place in the hills just above the Barneses. There he and Marianne and Lucy could live a country life, gardening, keeping a horse, dogs and cats, and even a tiny owl, which had flown in one day and decided to stay. They shared this house for a year with Ronald Macaulay, a Scots linguistics professor, and his wife and two children, and after that let out rooms to graduate students, to help with the rent.

But after two years, his contract at Pitzer was not renewed. It was the policy of the College not to keep visiting professors for more than two years. Such was the excuse made to obfuscate an act of stupidity, callousness and cruelty which one wishes were not typical of the academic mentality.

What is saddest and most embittering of all is that Rodgers had not only given—with his classes, public lectures, his Festival and his mere presence—what any college and community should covet: he also had given the last of his strength. He had felt ill during the summer of 1967 and, during a brief trip back to England, pain in his intestines became so acute that, on September 17th, he was operated on and a cancerous tumor was removed. Marianne flew to Colchester to be with him (Pitzer supplied the fare). He was not told of the malignancy, but the doctors informed Marianne that it would be a year before recovery could be certain. He regained his strength slowly and was unable to return to California until December 21st. But he was able to carry on his teaching through the second semester, with its Irish Festival—only to be told, toward the beginning of May, that he could not return.

Unsuccessful attempts were made to change the minds of the authorities. They were sorry, there was just no place for him. He and Marianne did not know what to do. She knew, though he did not, how ill he might still be. They hung on through the summer in Claremont, hoping that something might turn up. Finally he secured a part-time job at California State Polytechnic College, about ten miles away, and a grant from the Chapelbrook Foundation of Boston to prepare an edition of his B.B.C. tapes.

At Cal Poly he was assigned a class in the Bible—the closest he ever came to returning to the ministry, except for performing the marriage ceremony for a young Pitzer professor, a ceremony during which he surprised everyone by preaching an unscheduled sermon he had written that morning. I asked him what he taught his Bible class. "O," he said, "I tell them all the Irish stories." He liked his new students, and they him. Most of them were working their way through school, many were older than the normal college age, and he felt he had more rapport with them than with the young ladies of Pitzer. I never heard him complain about teaching, except that it tired him. I suppose he might not have minded the Bible class, but when the second quarter's schedule was drawn up, he was given a class in eighteenth-century English poetry. He had not thought much about eighteenth-century English poetry for forty years. He was so upset by this assignment that he could not bring himself to tell Marianne about it, and it was not in his nature to refuse it. But he never did get the chance to suffer the full indignity of having to go through with it.

Late in November 1968, he began to have trouble digesting his food. One of his last full nights of eating and drinking was at my apartment. He was pleased by the Bushmills, and the evening ended with singing and a fine display of Irish misogyny on his part—"Look at those two bitches on the couch, Darcy! Will you look at them! Bitches!"—but in good fun. After that evening he steadily declined, eating hardly anything at all during December. He entered the hospital just after the New Year.

It was the Los Angeles County General Hospital. As only a part-time employee at Cal-Poly, he did not qualify for medical insurance. The Los Angeles County General Hospital is the largest in the world. Except for certain emergency and contagious cases, no one goes there who can afford to go elsewhere. It is a charity hospital. He would not, of course, have been in such a place had he been in England or in Northern Ireland, nor even in the Republic of Ireland. He had to be in America to end his life in a ward crowded with the oppressed: blacks, Mexican-Americans, and W. R. Rodgers. I doubt that Rodgers himself cared about the hospital. He seemed to expect to die, and, being the man he was, he would sooner have died among wretches than rich men. The patient next to him was chained to the bed. He had been shot in the bowels running away from the police.

Marianne, thanks to a car loaned her by friends, the Douglas McClellans, was able to make the forty-mile trip to visit him each day, often with Lucy. She brought Bertie books and his favorite papers. My wife and I visited him twice, once before and once after his final operation. I had never seen a dying man, and I thought he looked rather well the first time. His books and papers were piled all about him. He talked about the other patients, especially about the poor fellow chained to his bed.

> A tether that held me to the hare
> Here, there, and everywhere.

The next time I saw him, he was almost too weak to speak. But he knew we were going to Ireland shortly, and he showed me a letter from his daughter Harden, which said that she was expecting us in Dublin, and he managed to write out a few names of people to look up. It was important to him, the missionary, that I do things properly.

Marianne and Lucy were with us on that last visit. Marianne forgot her umbrella near his bed, and when I went back into the room to fetch it for her, he was sitting up eating a pear, looking a bit stronger. I told Marianne. "You see," she said, "he wants me to think he's worse than he is. I'm sure he manages to look worse for me, so I'll baby him." That was for our benefit. The doctors had told her that he could live a few months at most. He died a few days later, at about 4:00 A.M., February 1.

A memorial service was held in Claremont. About a hundred people attended, including some whose interest in Rodgers I had been unaware of. The Colleges' chaplain, the Reverend E. C. Reckard, read from the scriptures, and there were personal statements by an old friend, Father Molaise Meehan, of the Order of St. Benedict, and by Barnes, Ronald Macaulay, and myself. Kate Barnes sang a song for him. We heard a tape of his voice, and a poem by Bert Meyers:

FOR W. R. RODGERS

I know a candle of a man
whose voice, meandering in a flame,
could make the shadows on the wall
listen to what he said.

> He's done. You'd need a broom
> to arouse him now. All things burn,
> writhe, shrink, dissolve, or drift away.
> Some men are words that warm a room.

Listening, I was aware of the effect which Rodgers had had on some of us, aware of a quality of blessedness about him. And it seemed that he could bless.

His ashes were flown to Belfast. My wife and I drove up from Dublin for the funeral, which began at the First Ballymacarrett Presbyterian Church, where Rodgers had gone as a child, and was to end with burial at Cloveneden Church, Loughgall. The Reverend W. G. M. Thompson, a friend from Rodgers's seminary days, conducted the services. Seamus Heaney, whom Rodgers had thought the most promising of young Irish poets, read selections from Rodgers's poetry, at Harden's request.

Then we drove to Loughgall and stood in the churchyard above the orchards and fields, on a bright March day, green all around and blue overhead. His sisters and his daughters by his first marriage were there, along with a few villagers who remembered Reverend Rodgers, and other friends, including Mrs. Patrick Kavanagh and Sean Mac Réamoinn, of Radio Éireann. Professor David Greene of Trinity College, Dublin, spoke a simple, eloquent eulogy, reminding us of Rodgers's devotion to the word.

After the burial, we stared at Rodgers's photograph in the vestibule of the church: the pale, intense young parson. That night we attended a wake at which his friends and family boisterously mourned him. I re-

membered the solemn service we had held for him in
Claremont. The two Americans who spoke then, Barnes
and I, had been barely able to get the words out. The
Irish were better at death than we because they, like
the man whose wake it was, were more conscious of
the circle of life. But we would all miss Bertie. At the
Claremont service, I had tried to put my word on him:

IN MEMORY OF W. R. RODGERS

He wrote once of a land
where all Is and nothing's Ought,
where there is neither yearning nor scorning,
but at night, the smell of morning.
He has left us for that land, and as he left,
there was the smell of morning.

I did not know you well, Bertie;
yet you always filled my glass to the brim.
And it stays full.
And looking into it now
I see your infant's face,
with all its veins showing,
with all its pain showing,
with a nice malice on its lips,
with humor and love in its eyes.
And when it got very late,
and one sensed the perfect coherence
in your perfect incoherence,
you would wag a finger and say,
"Do you know that I
was a Presbyterian minister
in County Armagh
for twelve long years!"
Ah Bertie, good-bye Bertie,
I do know this:
you ministered to me,

to anyone who could see
the truth of your verses
and of your Irish curses.

O Irish earth, receive the ashes
of another rebel, another exile.
America, you cannot claim him.
His land is neither here nor there.

Bibliography

Awake! And other poems. London: Secker & Warburg, 1941; New York: Harcourt, Brace, 1942, (under the title, *Awake! And Other Wartime Poems*).

Europa and the Bull. London: Secker & Warburg, 1952; New York: Farrar, Straus, and Cudahy, 1952.

Ireland in Colour. London: B. T. Batsford, 1957.

Essex Roundabout. Colchester: Benham and Company, 1963.

Note: The transcripts of Rodgers's radio portraits of Irish writers are being prepared by Mrs. Marianne Rodgers for publication by the B.B.C. *The Return Room*, which has been broadcast by the B.B.C. three times (1955, 1966, 1969), remains unpublished. An edition of the *Collected Poems*, edited by Dan Davin, is planned by Oxford University Press.